TRACING YOUR POOR ANCESTORS

FAMILY HISTORY FROM PEN & SWORD BOOKS

TRACING YOUR POOR ANCESTORS

A Guide for Family Historians

STUART A. RAYMOND

Pen & Sword
FAMILY HISTORY

First published in Great Britain in 2020
and reprinted in 2021 by
PEN AND SWORD FAMILY HISTORY
An imprint of
Pen & Sword Books Ltd
Yorkshire – Philadelphia

ISBN 978 1 52674 293 3

Typeset by Mac Style
Printed and bound in the UK by CPI Group (UK) Ltd,
Croydon, CR0 4YY.

Pen & Sword Books Limited incorporates the imprints of Atlas,
Archaeology, Aviation, Discovery, Family History, Fiction, History,
Maritime, Military, Military Classics, Politics, Select, Transport,
True Crime, Air World, Frontline Publishing, Leo Cooper, Remember
When, Seaforth Publishing, The Praetorian Press, Wharncliffe
Local History, Wharncliffe Transport, Wharncliffe True Crime
and White Owl.

For a complete list of Pen & Sword titles please contact

PEN & SWORD BOOKS LIMITED
47 Church Street, Barnsley, South Yorkshire, S70 2AS, England
E-mail: enquiries@pen-and-sword.co.uk
Website: www.pen-and-sword.co.uk

Or

PEN AND SWORD BOOKS
1950 Lawrence Rd, Havertown, PA 19083, USA
E-mail: Uspen-and-sword@casematepublishers.com
Website: www.penandswordbooks.com

CONTENTS

ACKNOWLEDGEMENTS

My major debt in writing this book is to the many historians who have investigated the poor, and whose works are cited throughout this book. My thanks too to the librarians and archivists in Trowbridge, Frome, and Chippenham, who have provided me with copies of those works, together with useful archival sources. The text has been read by Simon Fowler, and by one of my Pharos students who wishes to be anonymous; both have made useful comments, and saved me from errors. Any that remain are my responsibility, and I would be grateful if they could be brought to my attention.

PREFACE

Numerous records relating to the poor are found in The National Archives. Many are mentioned throughout this book, and National Archives references are given. Except where otherwise indicated, all class references cited here refer to classes of documents in the National Archives.

Chapter 1

PRELIMINARIES TO RESEARCHING THE POOR

The aim of this book is to help both family and local historians trace information about our poor ancestors in England and Wales between the sixteenth and the twentieth century. It is concerned not just with paupers – those dependent on the poor law – but also with the many poor who somehow just managed to survive (or perhaps died) without resorting to the overseer. What sources can be used to identify the poor? What information do they provide? Why were these sources created? Where can they be found? These are the basic questions dealt with here. The sources, and the information they contain, need to be placed in context. It may help, for example, if you realise that the government ran a migration agency in the 1830s to send workers from poor agricultural areas to the booming industrial areas of the North. Family and local history can only be properly understood if the wider historical context is also understood. The 'further reading' suggested throughout this book will lead you into deeper understanding of the forces which shaped our ancestors' lives.

This book concentrates attention on sources providing information about the poor. It assumes that you are already familiar with more general sources such as the census, the civil registers, and parish registers. If you are new to historical research, then you should read one of the many excellent general introductions currently available. There are far too many to list here, but the most comprehensive is:

- Herber, Mark. *Ancestral trails: the complete guide to British Genealogy and Family History.* 2nd ed. Sutton Publishing/Society of Genealogists, 2004.

See also:

- Few, Janet. *The Family Historian's Enquire Within*. 6th ed. Family History Partnership, 2014.
- Hey, David, Ed. *The Oxford Companion to Family and Local History*. 2nd ed. Oxford University Press, 2008.

Most historical research is now done on the internet, in record offices and in libraries. In the last two decades, the internet has transformed historical research, to such an extent that many family historians do not think of looking anywhere else. That is a bad mistake. While many original sources have been digitised, far more have not. Few recent books are online, although many older ones have been digitised.

You will probably use the internet before you visit libraries and record offices. It should be used with caution. For historians, it is an invaluable supplement to traditional sources of information. It is not a replacement for them, and it is important to be able to evaluate the reliability of particular websites. Useful introductory guides include:

- Christian, Peter. *The Genealogist's Internet: the essential guide to researching your family history online*. 5th ed. Bloomsbury, 2012.
- Paton, Chris. *Tracing your Family History on the Internet: a Guide for Family Historians*. 2nd ed. Pen & Sword, 2014.

A directory of relevant websites is provided by:

- Scott, Jonathan. *The Family History Web Directory*. Pen & Sword, 2015.

Record offices are warehouses for archives, which provide almost all the written evidence we need to trace our ancestors. Without them, books on family and local history could not be written, and the internet would be of little use to genealogists.

There are numerous record offices, both local and national. County record offices were originally created to house the records of Quarter Sessions, although nowadays they may also hold parish records, diocesan records and a wide range of private family and estate papers. For a full listing, see:

- Find An Archive in the UK and Beyond
  http://discovery.nationalarchives.gov.uk/find-an-archive

Nationally, the most significant record office for England and Wales is:

- The National Archives
  www.nationalarchives.gov.uk

Record offices usually have their own online catalogues listing their holdings. Many have also placed some or all of their catalogues on the National Archives' union catalogue:

- Discovery
  http://discovery.nationalarchives.gov.uk

For the holdings of University and College libraries (which, for example, hold the archives of many charities), see:

- Archives Hub
  https://archiveshub.jisc.ac.uk

Record offices within the London Metropolitan area have their own union catalogue:

- Aim 25: Archives in London and the M25 area
  https://aim25.com

You will also need to consult printed books. Until recently, books and original sources were generally housed in separate institutions, but nowadays many local studies collections include both, and The National Archives has an extensive library. There is an important distinction between them: original sources are unique, and therefore irreplaceable, whereas the print-run of most books is substantial, and they can easily be replaced. Many books are mentioned below; they can easily be obtained through your local public library or by purchase. Many of the older titles mentioned here (including a number of parliamentary papers) have been digitised and can be read online. For a union catalogue of digitised book websites, see:

- Just Free Books
  www.justfreebooks.info

The two most useful free book websites are:

- Internet Archive
  https://archive.org

- Hathi Trust Digital Library
  www.hathitrust.org

Many original sources have also been digitised, mainly on commercial sites, although some are available free on record office and other sites. The Discovery catalogue mentioned above identifies many sources held by The National Archives which have been digitised. The major commercial sites are:

- Ancestry
  www.ancestry.co.uk
- Find My Past
  www.findmypast.co.uk
- The Genealogist
  www.thegenealogist.co.uk

These sites are rivalled by the Church of Jesus Christ of Latter Day Saints (Mormons) Family History Library. Many digitised original sources can be freely consulted on its website:

- Family Search
  www.familysearch.org

Many other websites are listed by:

- Cyndi's List of Genealogy Sites on the Internet
  www.cyndislist.com

When consulting digitised documents online, do not rely on search boxes which say 'search here for everything'. Identify the specific source you want to check, for example 'settlement examinations', and restrict your search to that source. Remember to note where you found your information – not the website, but the record office holding the original document, and its reference number. Many digitised documents have been transferred between websites in recent years, whereas original documents are unlikely to change their locations.

In order to read early documents, some familiarity with archaic forms of handwriting, and with Latin (prior to 1733), may be necessary. Archaic handwriting is not difficult to read once you are familiar with the characters used. Beginners may find it useful to consult The National Archives tutorial:

- Palaeography: reading old handwriting, 1500 – 1800: A practical online tutorial
  www.nationalarchives.gov.uk/palaeography

Latin may be more difficult, although some documents follow a common form; for example, the Latin used in recognizances (see below, p.123) is almost always the same, and once you have read one you will know what to expect in all the others. For a useful tutorial, see:

- Learn Medieval Latin: an Introduction to Reading Medieval Latin Documents
  www.nationalarchives.gov.uk/latin/beginners

Parliamentary Papers

Not all original sources are in manuscript. There are numerous reports and papers dealing with the poor law, charities, and other topics among the Parliamentary Papers. The Reports of the 1832 and 1909 Royal Commissions on the Poor Law contain a huge mass of material on poor law administration, including statements from innumerable named witnesses. Reports on topics such as children in workhouses (1841) and the emigration of pauper children to Canada (1875) mention many names. 14,200 paupers are listed in an 1861 return of Paupers in Workhouses (partially indexed at **www.genuki.org.uk/big/eng/Paupers**, available on CD at **www.parishchest.com**, and digitised at **https://search.ancestry.co.uk/search/db.aspx?dbid=61439**). Annual reports from the Poor Law Commissioners and their successors summarise their work during each year.

Unfortunately, the means for identifying Parliamentary Papers containing information likely to be of use to family historians is limited. There are many guides, but they are not aimed at family historians. The most useful is probably:

- Powell, W.R. *Local history from blue books: a select list of the sessional papers of the House of Commons.* Helps for students of history 64. Historical Association, 1962.

Many (although not all) Parliamentary Papers are available at:

- British Parliamentary Publications
  https://archive.org/details/britishparliamentarypublications

A comprehensive collection of Parliamentary Papers is available online through academic libraries which subscribe to Proquest **http://proquest. libguides.com/parliamentary**. Many large research libraries also have collections of the original printed papers.

For further information on the Parliamentary Papers, see:

- Connected Histories: House of Commons Parliamentary Papers
  www.connectedhistories.org/resource.aspx?sr=pp

Chapter 2

THE HISTORY OF THE POOR

The Poor

'The poor you will always have with you'. Jesus's words are as true today as they were 2,000 years ago, although of course the nature of poverty has changed. The term 'poor' is a notoriously elastic concept. In earlier centuries, it included not just paupers and vagrants, but also many who did not apply for poor relief, but whose economic circumstances were nevertheless precarious. In eighteenth-century London, up to 60 per cent of the population experienced significant poverty at some point in their lives.[1] There were many varieties of poor; they were not an undifferentiated mass. We all have ancestors who were poverty-stricken, and perhaps had no shelter, few clothes, and little food. The Elizabethan poor laws of 1598 and 1601 were passed in the wake of many deaths from famine.

In the sixteenth and seventeenth century, population was increasing, but opportunities for employment did not keep pace, and price inflation far out-stripped wage inflation. The real value of labourers' wages fell by 50 per cent between 1500 and 1650.[2] The numbers of the poor steadily increased. In the 1520s, tax records suggest that the destitute constituted 13 per cent of the population of Babergh Hundred (Suffolk). The Dissolution of the Monasteries removed one of the major sources of poor relief. The monasteries had been obligated to give alms and to provide lodging houses for travellers. Furthermore, inflation took hold. Both food and rent became more expensive, while the real value of wages decreased, reaching a low point in the 1630s. At the same time, the rate of illegitimacy reached its peak, as did (probably) the amount of crime and vagrancy.[3] It has been argued that the primary impact of famine and dearth was not malnutrition and starvation, but rather the exacerbation of social tension within local communities.[4] That was not helped by the fact that the poor were very mobile. Perhaps two-fifths of the working population were dependent living-in servants.[5] Many of them moved on every year, but in doing so frequently encountered parish officers who regarded poor migrants as threats to poor rates – especially as long-distance migration increased significantly between 1580 and 1640.[6] Some Elizabethan and early Stuart surveys suggest the poor numbered between 20 and 30 per cent of the population. Gregory King's 1688 statistics suggest that no fewer than 51 per cent of the population were, as he put it, 'decreasing the wealth of the kingdom', and liable to become dependent upon poor relief.[7]

Sixteenth and seventeenth-century government did not fully understand the reason for what appeared to be the ever-increasing number of poor wandering vagrants. The Grand Jury at the Wiltshire Quarter Sessions in 1627 expressed the general puzzlement: it complained about 'the great inormatie & multitude of wandring persons which be soe great and doth dayly soe frequent us, but wheare the fault is we knowe not, but being soe publique if we should instance any particular personne we might seeme to be to severe, & to present all it were to be to much'.[8]

The government may not have understood the reasons for poverty, but it did understand all too clearly that it led to insecurity. There was a sizeable rural industrial proletariat, which was liable to become riotous at times of trade depression and harvest failure.[9] The poor played important roles in the four rebellions of the mid-sixteenth century. In the seventeenth century, they participated in the Midland Revolt of 1607, the Civil War, and Monmouth's rebellion. Famine, trade depression and enclosure frequently caused the poor to riot, to throw down fences, to stop the export of corn and to attack the supposed causes of their poverty. That continued throughout the eighteenth and into the nineteenth century. Luddism, for example, was a response to the introduction of machinery that seemed to threaten poor labourers. Much social legislation was designed to control the poor, and to reduce the danger of riot and rebellion. The seventeenth century also saw the beginnings of British settlement in North America. In the course of the century, perhaps 200,000 people emigrated, many of them poor.[10]

In the late eighteenth and early nineteenth century, the plight of the poor gradually worsened. In rural parishes, the gap between wealthy yeomen and the poor widened. In previous centuries, smallholders and small ratepayers – some of whom might be called on to serve in parish office – were aware that they too might at some stage need relief from the parish.[11] By 1800, that had largely ceased to be the case: the gap between agricultural labourers and ratepayers had become much wider. The custom of hiring by the year, and of single farm servants living in with their employer, was gradually disappearing.[12] The close connection between farmer and employee was also being severed. Those unlikely to need poor relief were much less sympathetic to those who did. The Industrial Revolution produced goods more efficiently. But it also led to the decline of cottage industries such as hand-spinning, framework knitting and handloom weaving, on which the poor relied. Enclosure took away access to land which had enabled the poor to be more self-reliant, and also improved the efficiency of farming, reducing the need for labour. The legal assault on gleaning (the gathering of grain missed by harvesters) did not help.[13] The economic effects of the Napoleonic wars exacerbated these problems, and the end of war in 1815 meant that many soldiers returned home, causing even more unemployment. The introduction of the threshing machine meant that agricultural labourers lost out. Their wages steadily decreased in value, and became so low that it became impossible for labouring families to survive on them. In 1797, in the rural Devon parish of Clyst St Mary, no labourer could 'maintain himself, his wife, and two children, on his earnings'.[14] The problem had ceased to be Elizabethan vagrancy; instead, it was that agricultural labourers were not being paid enough to support themselves and their families. By the early 1800s, 11 per cent of men were in receipt of some form of poor relief.[15] Some claimed that parish roads had never been in a better state of repair than in the 1830s, because pauper labourers were forced to work on them.[16] After around 1795, the lists of paupers which many parishes kept changed their character; instead of being primarily lists of widows, the aged and children, the names of men unable to earn a liveable wage began to predominate.[17] The amount spent on poor relief grew rapidly. Where £2,000,000 had been spent in 1783–5, £8,000,000 was spent in 1818.[18]

The Victorians perhaps had a better understanding of the plight of the poor than the Elizabethans. Nevertheless, all too frequently the poor were blamed for their own plight. The terms 'labourer' and 'poor' were frequently regarded as synonymous, as most labourers needed support from the parish at some stage in their lives. Life cycle conditions such as sickness, widowhood, orphanhood and old age caused many to apply for poor relief.[19] The decline of rural industry in the face of more efficient competition, and trade depressions in new industries – such as cotton manufacture at the time of the American Civil War – resulted in much unemployment during the Industrial Revolution. Agricultural labourers received starvation wages. Some became vagrants, begging their livelihood. Others became criminals, living off the proceeds of ill-gotten gains. Widows, orphans and the sick were sometimes cared for by charities.

The Poor Law

In principle, government at all levels – Privy Council, Parliament, Quarter Sessions, and parish – accepted the necessity of relieving paupers. Nevertheless, the authorities thought that claims of poverty were frequently not genuine. Beggars in particular were suspect; consequently, opposition to indiscriminate almsgiving led to it being banned in some Tudor legislation. The poor, in the eyes of the elite, constituted the criminal classes, the people most likely to be charged with felonies or misdemeanors. Nevertheless, there were the respectable poor: the aged, widows, orphaned children and the sick. Destitute 'deserving poor', who suffered through no fault of their own, had to be provided for, if grudgingly. Maimed soldiers were frequently granted pensions by Quarter Sessions.

Criteria such as church attendance, industriousness, sobriety and deference helped determine who was 'deserving'.[20] Able-bodied paupers attracted great suspicion. It was frequently assumed that they could easily enter service, despite the fact that many were thrown out of work during trade depressions. They were thought not to need poor relief. Yet denial of poor relief was likely to lead to increasing numbers thronging the roads looking for work. Other travellers included ship-wrecked mariners travelling home, slaves who had escaped their North African captors, Londoners on their way to pick hops in Kent, Irish labourers looking for seasonal work and poor students on their way to Oxford and Cambridge. They were all in danger of being regarded as vagrants, who were definitely not thought of as 'deserving'. They were perceived as a danger to settled society, and were the targets of much vicious legislation. They were regarded as only fit to be whipped and 'removed' to their place of settlement. 'Settlement', as we will see, was a word with a special meaning, which attracted considerable attention from parish officers, Justices of the Peace, lawyers and the poor who had to negotiate with parish bureaucracy for their poor relief.

Reformers in the eighteenth and nineteenth century focused their attention on the cost of relief, rather than the underlying social and economic changes which were taking place. The Poor Law Commissioners were so concerned about the need to reduce the relief given to able-bodied poor that they almost completely ignored the people who actually needed workhouses – the sick, the aged and the children. Bishop Watson (Bishop of Llandaff, 1782–1816), in one of his less Christian moments, characterized the agricultural labourer as 'perverse, stupid, and illiterate'.[21] In 1601 the unworthy poor were vagrants and migrants. By 1834, all dependent poor were regarded as unworthy. They had become 'strangers who menaced the respectable through their disorderly lives'.[22] The Victorian middle class discussion of 'Hodge' knew little about the actual lives of the poor.[23] Both old and new poor laws, despite the rhetoric of relieving distress, in practice gave the elite, meeting in parish vestry or at Board of Guardians meetings, a very convenient means of exercising control over their humbler neighbours.[24]

The poor themselves had a strong sense of entitlement to public support if all else failed, although this was based on political, moral and religious sentiment rather than on the law. Poor relief was not, however, their only resource. Access to land before the enclosure movement meant that they could collect their own fuel, perhaps feed a pig in the woodland, and take full advantage of other natural resources. Pawnbrokers might be of assistance when they were short of cash. The theft of produce from

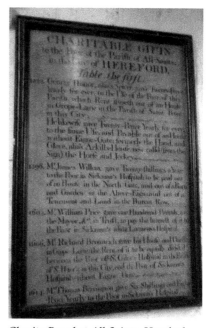

Charity Board at Poole.

Charity Board at All Saints, Hereford.

someone's garden might, with luck, not be noticed. The theft of a sheep might have more serious consequences, but the culprit would probably not be detected. The poor placed great reliance on casual charity, which was much more important than governmental provision of poor relief. Indeed, under the old poor law, the relief that was granted by overseers was frequently merely intended to supplement assistance provided by family and friends.[25] Many testators made small bequests to the poor of their parish. In some parishes, it was decades before the provisions of the Elizabethan poor laws were fully implemented. It was frequently not expected that parish relief would be sufficient of itself to maintain the pauper.[26] Other makeshifts were also likely to be needed. Charity remained important – although magisterial attempts to increase poor rates were likely to result in ratepayers reducing or withdrawing their charitable giving.

Charity came from many sources. It did not simply consist of handouts from the upper classes. Kinship networks enabled some poor to survive. The poor helped each other to navigate crises. Reciprocity and neighbourliness were crucial.[27] Consequently, many poor did not appeal to the parish, or enter the workhouse. Those options really were the last resort.

The elite took little interest in the opinions of the poor, and knew little of their worries, their priorities, or the constraints under which they suffered. Bishop Watson evidently thought there was little point in asking their opinions about anything. They did, however, have opinions, which were expressed on the infrequent occasions when they wrote letters. Pauper letters to overseers sometimes survive; despite their obsequious tone, they provide enlightening evidence about paupers' lives. The freest expressions of the opinions of the poor are to be found in the letters of poor emigrants. Many had discovered lands that they considered to be flowing with milk and honey. In 1836, John Walden, formerly of Climping (Sussex) wrote home to say 'I hope you will not fail in coming, for I wish I had come ten years before I did; for here we can get a good living and be independent of any one.'[28] These letters make it clear that the quality of family life was the top priority of the poor – a priority which the poor law at home took little account of. The need for land and some livestock was another almost overwhelming concern. The poor at home frequently lost access to land as the result of enclosure. Its availability in the colonies was frequently emphasised by (formerly) poor emigrants. Many emigrants lauded their ability to hunt game. At home, that was called poaching, and was liable to result in an appearance at Quarter Sessions. Employment was of lesser concern, although some commented that servants in the colonies were scarce, and could expect to hold secure positions. At home, the decline of the practice of servants living-in on annual contracts in the late eighteenth- and early nineteenth century had meant the gradual erosion of security for the labouring classes.

Security was one of government's major concerns. As we have seen, it acknowledged that security for the poor meant security for the government as well. The humanitarian instinct was also important: the Church insisted that genuine poverty should be relieved. There was little difference on that point between Roman Catholics and Protestants. But old medieval attitudes were changing: charity was not to be indulged in simply for the salvation of the giver, but should aim to reform the recipients. It should be provided by governmental authority, and should be effective. Sixteenth-century humanists thought that governments were capable of eliminating poverty, and that they had a duty to engage in social engineering.[29] Such attitudes underlay much Elizabethan and early Stuart social legislation.

Legislation was driven, not by the central government, but by the reaction of local authorities in towns and cities to the problem of poverty. Many devised their own solutions.[30] In mid-sixteenth-century London, city authorities built four 'hospitals' catering for different purposes: Christ's Hospital for foundling children, Bridewell for rogues and vagabonds, St Thomas's and St Bartholomew's for the sick and lame. The cost was met by the first poor rate levied in England.[31] Puritan magistrates in cities such as Norwich, Salisbury and Dorchester similarly developed comprehensive schemes of poor relief. In 1619, 100 vagrant children from London were sent to join the first permanent English settlement in Virginia.[32] This was the first example of local government using emigration as a means of relieving poverty. Parliament first legislated for the transportation of convicts in 1597. Many of the legislative solutions to the problem of poverty – for example, the badging of the poor[33] – were tried out locally before being incorporated in Acts of Parliament.

Under the Tudors, various legislative attempts were made to provide for the poor, and to tackle the perceived curse of vagrancy. The parish was the obvious unit of government to undertake the task; indeed, a portion of the parish incumbent's tithe was supposed to be given to the poor.[34] In practice, that proved to be insufficient. An Act of 1552 created a 'Collector of [voluntary] Alms' in each parish. The Act required parishes to keep a register of licensed poor, and prohibited begging completely. In 1563, contributions became compulsory. In 1572, 'collectors' became 'overseers', authorised to assess and levy poor rates. The names of the 'aged, decayed, and impotent [unable to work]' poor had to be registered, and overseers were expected to conduct monthly 'views and searches' of the poor. Beggars were to be licensed if parishes could not provide for them. Vagrants could be whipped or burnt through the ear, and their children were to be apprenticed. In 1576, overseers were instructed to provide stock to 'set the poor on work'; houses of correction were to be erected to punish those who refused to work.

The great Elizabethan Act of 1598, confirmed in 1601, consolidated all these measures, and laid the foundation of the poor law until 1834.[35] Each parish had a duty to provide relief for the impotent poor, work for the able-bodied who could not find it, and punishment for vagrants and the idle. Pauper children were to be apprenticed once they were old enough. It was sometimes necessary to board out orphans before apprenticeship.

Poor rates were to be levied to meet costs. Parish overseers of the poor were to be appointed by Justices of the Peace. Churchwardens became *ex officio* overseers. Poverty was seen as a local issue, to be solved at a local level. Overseers determined for themselves (subject to the oversight of Justices of the Peace) who was to be relieved, and what relief was to be granted. If they thought fit, they could withhold relief. The Acts ignored the fact that some parishes, especially in cities, had many wealthy inhabitants, while others were primarily inhabited by the poor, and thus less able to provide adequate relief. In the North, administrators faced a different problem: parishes were huge, made up of many townships sometimes unwilling to cooperate with each other. It was not until 1662 that the problem was remedied by making such townships responsible for administering the poor law by themselves.

In practice, the Elizabethan Acts merely provided the framework for a multiplicity of different systems of poor relief. The same, incidentally, can be said of the 1834 Act.[36] There was no consistency in decision-making either between parishes, or, over time, within parishes. It is not clear how long it took for the Elizabethan Acts to be fully implemented, although by the 1690s most parishes probably had some sort of welfare system in place.[37]

The legal framework provided by the Elizabethan Acts did enable parishes to establish an effective, comprehensive, and flexible system for the relief of the deserving poor. That, however, was peripheral to the prime purpose of the legislation. The intention had been to provide work for the unemployed, and thus end the need for poor relief.[38] Overseers never satisfactorily solved the conundrum involved in meeting that aim. If economic conditions meant that work was not profitable, how could they make it so? The able-bodied only sought relief when trade was slack. But slack trade meant that any goods they produced could not be sold, and therefore costs could not be recovered.

The Elizabethan poor law was originally based on citizen participation; the gradual accretion of statutes helped to turn it into an enormous bureaucratic maze, creating much business for lawyers. In eighteenth-century London in particular, the system became a rules-based bureaucracy, increasingly administered by a 'cadre of salaried officers and professional lawyers and justices'.[39] Hence much paper was created for us to consult.

The parish was not the only unit of government to be involved in poor law administration. Quarter Sessions, and the Privy Council, also played important roles. The Privy Council was particularly active in the 1630s, during Charles I's 'personal rule'. It required regular reports from Quarter Sessions on poor law activity;[40] those reports (among the SP classes in The National Archives) tell us most of what we know about the early relief system, although they rarely record names. The role of Justices of the Peace, and of Quarter Sessions, was to enforce the law, and to adjudicate disputes. They ensured that paupers received relief when overseers were unwilling to give it, and they decided which parish was responsible for providing relief in individual cases.

In the seventeenth century, poor rates became increasingly common. By 1660 they were being levied in a third of English parishes. By the end of the century they were universal, except in Wales.[41] The money raised was used to provide a variety of services, greatly expanding the simple concept of relief embodied in the Elizabethan legislation.[42] The unemployed and the sick might be given a cash dole. The impotent might be given clothes, shoes, food or fuel; their rent might be paid; they might be given weekly pensions. There might be payments for the foster care of village orphans, or for the support of illegitimate children. Small premiums and other expenses were incurred in binding pauper apprentices, and in removing others, such as pregnant husbandless women, who were likely to become burdens on the rates. Some parishes erected workhouses, so that the poor could be set on work. Stock such as flax or wool, together with spinning wheels or other tools, might have to be purchased. Setting the poor on work was central to poor law philosophy. All of these expenses should have been recorded in overseers' accounts (which may or may not note paupers' names).[43] There were attempts to insist on the 'workhouse test', whereby paupers would be refused relief unless they entered the workhouse. However, that was rarely enforced for any length of time:[44] it was impractical, despite the fact that it subsequently formed one of the theoretical bases for the new poor law after 1834.

As the system developed, a number of other problems came to the fore.[45] Firstly, who might legitimately claim relief in a particular parish? Secondly, how could relief be restricted to the 'deserving' poor? Thirdly, how could those responsible for distributing relief be held to account, and prevented from being over-generous?

The answer to the first question depended on the notion of 'settlement'. It was implicit in the Elizabethan legislation that everyone had a parish of 'settlement', to which they could return if they became 'indigent' [destitute]. That parish was responsible for paying relief. Determining settlement was not, however, an easy matter. The rules for doing so were not formalised until after the Restoration of Charles II; they are outlined in Chapter 4. The Act of Settlement 1662 has been described as being 'of dubious origins and ramshackle structure'.[46] In 1776, Adam Smith commented that 'there is scarce a poor man in England of forty years of age... who has not in some part of his life felt himself cruelly oppressed by this ill-contrived law of settlements.'[47] Nevertheless, much of it remained on the statute book until as late as 1948. Parish officers spent a lot of time checking up on the 'un-settled' in their parishes.[48] The law threatened even those who were not claiming relief: those who were thought 'likely to be chargeable' could be removed under the 1662 Act. Many were. Until the end of the eighteenth century, the rules for settlement became ever more restrictive of the poor.[49]

The settlement examination, made before a Justice of the Peace, is now a key document for family historians (see below, p.70–71). It enabled Justices to determine whether a pauper should be removed. Removal, however, was an uncertain remedy. Parishes which resorted to it indiscriminately were liable to find themselves faced with substantial unexpected costs, without necessarily achieving their objective.[50] In practice, only those who threatened to become a charge on parishes were removed. Most of those mentioned in settlement examinations and removal orders were women or married men with children. Very few settlement examinations were taken from men who were actually employed. Young men offered useful and employable labour and were welcomed, not removed. The threat of removal might be used to deter applications for poor relief, but it was quite another matter to implement the threat.

There were other means of dealing with poor migrants, such as paying minimal relief, refusing it altogether, or persuading paupers to move on of their own accord, perhaps even paying them to do so. Removal was not necessarily seen as the most appropriate remedy for the unemployed.

In nineteenth-century Stockport, for example, it was argued that the recovery of the town's industry from trade depression would be seriously damaged if workers who had been temporarily laid off were removed: there would be no workers to employ when trade improved.[51]

The pressures faced by overseers sometimes enabled paupers to negotiate the terms of their relief with the overseers. When Thomas Morris, who lived in Sawbridgeworth (Hertfordshire), but was settled in St Martin, Vintry, London, fell ill in 1816 and sought help with his rent, the St Martin's overseers felt bound to provide it, as otherwise the Sawbridgeworth overseers might have him removed – in which case they would have to provide relief for his seven children.[52]

Overseers operated under the supervision of Justices of the Peace, who appointed them, audited their accounts and ensured that they acted within the law. Justices settled rating and settlement disputes, and could order the relief of individuals. Their activities are recorded in Quarter Sessions order books and sessional rolls.[53] Some justices kept a record of their own activities in 'justicing books'.

In the half century before the introduction of the new poor law, magistrates and overseers were increasingly anxious to find ways of reducing expenditure on poor relief, while avoiding increases in agricultural wages. The 'Speenhamland' system, adopted by Berkshire magistrates, supplemented low wages by a dole to ensure that labourers had enough to live on. Many parishes adopted similar measures. Some used the roundsman system, in which local masters employed paupers in turn. The labour rate system, whereby the parish paid a dole to able-bodied paupers, but sold their labour to local farmers, was another variation. By 1824, no fewer than 41 per cent of parishes offered relief to supplement low wages.[54]

Despite the emphasis historians have placed on subsidising poorly paid labourers, only 20 per cent of paupers were able-bodied men at the beginning of the nineteenth century.[55] Life expectancy was low; there were numerous widows and orphans. A woman's wage was rarely likely to be sufficient to support a family, so most widows with young children were dependent on poor relief. Many other paupers were elderly: in Abson and Wick (Gloucestershire) no fewer than 50 per cent of the elderly were in receipt of relief on their deaths.[56]

Rates, however, increased inexorably. Unfortunately, politicians and magistrates tended to concentrate their attention on the expense, rather than the cause, and blamed the victims for their inability to find work. Consequently, the idea of the workhouse, which had been implicit in earlier legislation, was gradually developed.

In the seventeenth century, government decided that workhouse discipline could impose morality, and at the same time provide paupers with work. In the 1630s a number of urban parishes reported to the Privy Council that they had established workhouses to give the poor employment.[57] During the Commonwealth, a Corporation of the Poor was established in London, in order to construct workhouses and Houses of Correction. That came to an end when Charles II was restored in 1660, but provision for workhouses in London was made by the 1662 Settlement Act. The London Corporation was fully revived in 1696, and became the model for Corporations of the Poor in other towns and cities, Bristol[58] and Exeter leading the way in 1696 and 1697. By 1711, fifteen city Corporations of the Poor had been established.[59]

The urban example was soon adopted in many rural parishes. From around 1710, many individual parishes built their own workhouses. In 1722, Knatchbull's Act (sometimes known as the Workhouse Test Act) authorised parishes to open workhouses, and to combine with neighbouring parishes to do so.[60] Overseers were permitted to refuse outdoor relief, and to insist that relief was only available within the workhouse, in return for labour where the pauper was capable. This test was frequently applied in eighteenth-century workhouses;[61] paupers could choose either to enter the workhouse, or to receive no relief. The Act also permitted parishes to farm their poor out to contractors, who would provide food, clothing, accommodation and even cash doles in return for a fixed price per pauper per week. By 1750, perhaps 600 mostly small workhouses had been established.[62] Their numbers steadily increased; by 1777 there were 1,916 parish workhouses, housing over 90,000 paupers;[63] in 1803, 3,765 workhouses were counted, housing perhaps a fifth of paupers receiving regular relief.[64]

Gilbert's Act 1782 provided further enabling powers. Under it, workhouses were to be erected solely for the care of the impotent poor, not for deterrent purposes. The able-bodied were not to be admitted. The Act set out rules on matters such as the size of unions, their government and administration. Unions of parishes created under its auspices were to be governed by boards of elected guardians, under a visitor, rather than overseers.[65] About eighty 'Gilbert unions' were established. These were the prototypes of the unions established in 1834, but most remained outside of the remit of the central Poor Law authorities until 1868. Their workhouses were immortalised in the words of George Crabbe's 1810 poem, *The Borough*:

Your plan I love not. With a number you
Have placed your poor, your pitiable few;
There, in one house throughout their lives to be,
The pauper-palace which they hate to see:
That giant-building, that high bounding wall,
Those bare-worn walks, that lofty thundering hall!
That large clock, which tolls each dreaded hour,
Those gates and locks and all those signs of power:
It is a prison, with a milder name,
Which few inhabit without dread or shame.

In the early nineteenth century, as we have seen, the old poor law continued to be under increasing pressure. There were various attempts at reform, but it was not until after the Royal Commission on the Poor Law reported in 1832 that the Elizabethan legislation was replaced. The Poor Law Amendment Act 1834 created an entirely new system, and swept away much of the old administrative structure. It established unions of parishes, with elected Boards of Guardians, and salaried relieving officers, to administer poor relief. The Guardians were constrained to act within strict procedural and accounting rules under the direct supervision of Assistant Commissioners and of the Commission itself;[66] they did not have the independence of the old overseers. They were expected to employ a workhouse master and various other professional officers; the old amateur approach was to cease. All applicants for relief were supposed to be admitted to much larger workhouses, where work could be more effectively supervised. The reformers made a determined effort to redefine terms relating to the lower classes. Poverty was reconceptualised. Officialdom began to view the 'deserving poor', and the paupers, almost as two separate classes. In some circles, dependency on poor relief began to be viewed almost as a crime. When Henry Fielding, in 1751, made his proposal to build a new Middlesex workhouse for the poor, he published it in his *Enquiry into the Causes of the late Increase of Robberies*.[67]

The principle of 'less eligibility' changed the entire ethos of poor relief. It required that recipients of poor relief should be materially worse off than the poorest labourers in employment. Out-relief, in theory, was only supposed to be given 'in cases of sudden urgent necessity'; in cases of sickness, accident or infirmity; to widows in the first six months of widowhood; to widows with legitimate children only; to the dependants of imprisoned convicts; to the families of soldiers, sailors or marines; to the resident family of a non-resident head, and to pay burial costs.[68]

Otherwise, all applicants had to pass the 'workhouse test' in order to prove their need for relief. Theoretically, relief could only be obtained by entering the workhouse. The theory was never fully realised. The attempt to realise it did, however, have consequences. Paupers were severely disciplined, the poor were marginalised and the poor law ceased to bind rich and poor together.[69]

Each union was expected to have its own workhouse, where the principle of 'less eligibility' could be inflicted on recipients of relief. The purpose of the Workhouse was to keep paupers out, and to deny relief to all but those who had no alternative. The discipline to be imposed on workhouse inmates was intended to be unacceptable to all but the most destitute. The relief provided was to be the minimum necessary to sustain life.

In practice, many Guardians gave as much out-relief as was possible while staying within the law, despite pressure from the Poor Law Commissioners and their successors. A poor law inspector commented in 1856 that 'with scarcely an exception, the tendency everywhere is to substitute outdoor relief for indoor relief whenever the Guardians may legally do so.'[70] Perhaps two-thirds of those granted relief by Guardians continued to receive out-relief, consisting of a small dole and perhaps a loaf of bread or other necessities.[71] Sometimes local officials manipulated their records to avoid problems with Whitehall. For example, highway rates could be levied to employ paupers on the roads. Technically, that was not out-relief, and therefore did not need to be reported to the Poor Law Commission.

Design for a Workhouse, from the 1st report of the Poor Law Commissioners.

Gate of the Oracle Workhouse, Reading, c.1910.

Out-relief was cheaper for the Guardians than insisting on the Workhouse. In any case, there were insufficient workhouses to accommodate the able-bodied unemployed, especially when fluctuations in trade led to high unemployment. In the 1840s, a time of serious depression, outdoor paupers outnumbered inmates of workhouses by seven to one.[72] The idea of deterrence was clearly irrelevant when the American Civil War caused mass unemployment in the cotton factories of Lancashire. It became obvious that pauperism could not be cured by prescribing the workhouse.[73] It was not, however, until the 1880s that the word 'unemployed' came into common usage,[74] reflecting the increasing awareness that the unemployed could not be held accountable for the lack of employment opportunities.

The 1834 Act resulted in considerable opposition, especially in the North. The anger and disbelief among the poor which greeted the advent of the New Poor Law was due to the fact that out-relief had become increasingly vital to their household economies. They had lost access to land when parishes were enclosed, and the Industrial Revolution had destroyed their cottage industries. The withdrawal of out-relief was seen as an attack on the final prop which held their economy of makeshifts together.[75]

There was also much opposition in more influential circles, especially when abuse became notorious. When paupers at Andover Workhouse were driven by hunger to gnaw the putrid bones which they were supposed to be crushing to make fertiliser, Victorian society was scandalised. A Parliamentary Select Committee forced action, and in 1847 the Poor Law Commission was replaced by the Poor Law Board, consisting of four ministers. In practice, the Board never met, but its President became a government minister answerable in Parliament. In

1871, its duties were absorbed by the Local Government Board, which in turn was absorbed by the Ministry of Health in 1919.

The new poor law survived for a century. It was administered by elected Boards of Guardians, answerable to the ratepayers, who both elected them and paid the cost of poor relief. Guardians were mostly minor gentry and small businessmen (especially shopkeepers). Justices of the Peace sat *ex officio* until 1894. Many of the elected Guardians were primarily interested in costs, rather than in providing relief. They were generally happy to implement 'less eligibility', and Boards of Guardians did produce the hefty savings on poor relief that had been sought. In 1830, £7,300,000 had been spent; by 1856, the figure was £4,600,000.[76] Guardians were, however, less enthusiastic about having to find money for the extensive building projects needed to achieve the Commissioners' aims. Many were reluctant to expend ratepayers' money on new buildings, and the Commissioners had no powers to insist on expenditure. Consequently, it took a long time to build all the workhouses required. Nevertheless, many were completed. Union workhouses were large institutions, not the small parish workhouses of yesteryear. By 1839, there were 585 unions in existence, with 252 new workhouses and 175 old ones. Sixty-seven new workhouses were under construction.[77] The number of workhouses rapidly declined as the old parochial workhouses were closed down. But the size of the new buildings meant that many more places became available for paupers. By 1850, the number of workhouses in the south and east had declined from 2,150 in 1830 to just 750, but their capacity had increased ten-fold.[78] It was not until the 1870s that every union had its own workhouse.

Under the 1834 Act, parishes ceased to be the prime unit of poor law administration. However, overseers retained some residual duties, such as meeting the cost of their own paupers, providing relief in kind, admitting paupers to workhouses,[79] chasing the fathers of illegitimate children for maintenance and asking justices to conduct settlement examinations. Therefore, parish records should not be neglected after 1834. Some functions were transferred to unions by the Union Chargeability Act 1865, although parish overseers continued to levy the rates which supported unions until 1925.

The concept of settlement was similarly retained, with minor changes. Removal of paupers between parishes within unions ceased. Settlement examinations, removal orders and related documents continued to be written. A new document, a notice of chargeability and removal, had to be sent to the receiving parish when a pauper was removed.

Oliver Twist and Mr. Bumble in the Workhouse.

The workhouse was run by a master appointed by the Guardians. He was assisted by a matron – frequently his wife. The relieving officer was responsible for admitting paupers and dealing with out-relief. Unions employed a variety of other staff. The Clerk to the Board dealt with minutes and correspondence, the treasurer dealt with finances, medical officers and nurses looked after the sick, the chaplain was responsible for spiritual care, the schoolmaster or mistress taught the children, and the porter controlled the gate.

There were some outstanding examples of enlightened Boards and workhouse masters. Some made great efforts to educate the children in their charge, and to care for the infirm and elderly. Masters could inflict severe punishments on refractory paupers, but one master, Daniel Pickett, commented that he had not 'punished half-a-dozen people or taken more than two before the guardians, during my 40 years in poor law service'. He did not 'believe in too much power being allotted to one man', and his punishment book was covered in dust due to his failure to use it.[80]

Pickett was not typical. For one union with an imaginative and caring staff, there were perhaps six where staff were unresponsive to the needs of paupers, and where Guardians were primarily concerned to keep rates low.[81] Paupers were entitled to complain – but rarely bothered, as complaints were merely referred back to the Guardians.

The Poor Law Commissioners showed little interest in medical care. The legislation of 1834 barely mentioned it, apart from authorising Boards of Guardians to appoint medical officers. There was no plan to build workhouse infirmaries. Nevertheless, nothing proved more subversive of the principles of 1834 than illness and infirmity. Provision of medical service to the poor developed in response to need, rather than ideology. In 1842, the Commission issued a general medical order regulating the conduct of infirmaries and medical officers. At first there were many problems. Infirmary buildings were frequently dirty, over-crowded, and unsuitable for their purpose. Guardians were reluctant to spend money on them. Nurses were unqualified, and, indeed, frequently paupers themselves. There was perpetual conflict between medical officers and relieving officers over the need for medical relief. In 1852, however, it was recognised that inability to pay for medical problems created an entitlement to free treatment.[82] Union infirmaries became ubiquitous. The persistence of medical officers in advocating reform resulted in steady improvement, and 'turned paupers into patients'.[83] In terms of the principle of 'less eligibility', infirmaries were extravagant; their patients were better off than the great mass of the poor who did not claim poor relief. Ultimately, many workhouse infirmaries became NHS hospitals.[84]

Sir Edwin Chadwick, poor law commissioner.

The new poor law system established in 1834 took several decades to be fully implemented. It was resisted not only by the poor, but also by some parishes. Parishes had to adopt the Act; some refused to do so for decades.[85] The system was overseen by the Poor Law Commission; their Assistant Commissioners (later termed inspectors) travelled the country overseeing the activities of unions on its behalf. Their first task was to create Poor Law Unions.[86] Ideally, they would be centred on a market town and its surrounding rural parishes. Some covered large areas: the Southwell Union, for example, included sixty parishes. In cities, however, unions might cover only a few parishes: Poplar Union included the parishes of Poplar, Blackwell, Bromley, and Stratford by Bow.[87] The Commissioners were anxious to ensure that unions were sufficiently large to be able to pay for a sizeable workhouse. They did not necessarily follow existing boundaries; the Mere Union, for example, included parishes in three counties: Dorset, Somerset and Wiltshire. Those unions which existed before 1834 (see above) were mostly amalgamated into the new system. A handful of London unions remained separate until 1867.

The Commissioners thought that the harshness of treatment in workhouses would deter the idle and act as a spur to the industry and enterprise of the able-bodied poor. As has already been noted, the 1832 report ignored the needs of the young, the old, and the sick, who, in practice, formed the majority of workhouse occupants. Indeed, in 1838 almost half of workhouse inmates were children.[88] After the first decade or so, and except in times of serious distress, able-bodied males (other than vagrants – known as 'casuals') disappeared from workhouses. Two-thirds of adult paupers in workhouses in both 1871 and 1900 were females.[89]

The children, too, gradually disappeared, as we will see. Workhouses became homes to the aged, the decrepit, and the geriatric, and to those who were temporarily or permanently sick. Returns of 1861 and 1871 reveal that a fifth of inmates had been resident for over five years. The proportion of resident lunatics increased from 1% in 1842 to 8% in 1910.[90] By the 1890s, poor law workhouses had morphed into infirmaries, asylums, and old people's homes. The principle of less eligibility obviously had no relevance to most of those who actually used the workhouses, but the fact was ignored by many Victorian legislators and Guardians. 'Discipline' had to be imposed, although admittedly it was gradually relaxed towards the end of the century.

In 1839, perhaps a third of workhouse inmates were children.[91] Initially, many London unions continued the practice of 'baby farming', whereby substantial private institutions in the country were paid to foster young children. That came to an end after 1849, when disaster struck Mr Drouet's establishment for pauper children at Tooting. It housed some 1,400 children when cholera broke out and killed 180 children. After the furore, Dickens commented that the epidemic 'broke out in Mr Drouet's farm for children, because it was brutally conducted, vilely kept, preposterously inspected, dishonestly defended, a disgrace to a Christian community, and a stain upon a civilised land'. The practice of using such establishments ceased almost immediately.[92]

Initially, most workhouse children were taught in the workhouse.[93] The Poor Law Commission required every union to provide schooling for pauper children, with a salaried schoolmaster or mistress. But many Guardians were reluctant to spend money on education. Consequently, workhouse schooling was often of questionable quality, especially in the early days. Legislation in 1845 requiring pauper apprentices to be able to read their own indentures resulted in some improvement. So did the 1846 creation of a central fund to pay the salaries of workhouse teachers; henceforth, their pay was to be based on their competence. From the 1850s, industrial training was increasingly emphasised. In rural areas, farm schools could be almost self-supporting. Guardians gradually came to realise that the principle of 'less eligibility' was irrelevant when dealing with children; rather, they needed 'dis-pauperization'.[94]

The Poor Law Commission and its successors emphasised the need to keep children away from adult paupers, for fear of their 'contaminating influence'. Considerable efforts were made to keep the two categories apart, sometimes resulting in the construction of schools at some distance from workhouses. From 1849, a few urban unions united with others to establish separate District Schools, which offered economies of scale, and where a wider range of trades could be taught. By the 1890s, London had five District Schools, formed by fifteen unions.[95] These, however, attracted considerable criticism, and were pejoratively termed 'barrack schools'. They were expensive to run, and disease-prone.

After 1862, Guardians could board their children in privately run 'Certified Schools'. Catholics in particular took advantage of this provision to ensure that their children escaped the Protestantism of the poor law establishment. A few children were sent to training ships, where they could learn seamanship. Those ships which took boys from poor law institutions are listed by Higginbotham.[96]

The 1870 Education Act gave the Guardians joint responsibility with School Boards for the education of the poor. An 1873 Act made education a mandatory condition of outdoor relief.[97] Many smaller unions sent their children to the new elementary (Board) schools, closing their own schools. The value of the larger workhouse schools was increasingly questioned; they made little provision for creating a family-like atmosphere. From the 1890s, some unions removed their children from workhouses altogether. Instead, they built 'cottage homes', where small groups could be brought up together in a more family-like atmosphere. Meanwhile, the Local Government Board banned the provision of accommodation for children in new workhouses. In 1913 it required the Guardians to build special institutions for them, or to foster them out. This requirement was strengthened in 1915, when Guardians were instructed not to allow children over three years of age to live in workhouses for more than six weeks.

Foster care was also developing. It began officially in 1869, when a number of unions undertook trials. Many unions created boarding-out committees (their minutes may be useful), in which women played major roles. By 1877, there were 9,248 children boarded out.[98] By the end of the nineteenth century, half of English unions were sending their children to foster homes.[99]

There were also many elderly inmates in workhouses, no longer capable of earning a living. In theory, they were the responsibility of their families. Minutes frequently record Guardians seeking maintenance orders requiring children to support their elderly parents.

The chronically ill were another major category of inmates. We have already discussed the problems facing workhouse infirmaries. A damning series of articles in the *Lancet* brought the plight of London's sick to the attention of the government, and led to the Metropolitan Poor Act 1867.[100] The Act acknowledged for the first time that the State had the responsibility to provide hospitals for the poor, and marked an important step toward the creation of the National Health Service. The government used its provisions to create the Metropolitan Asylums Board, which provided large specialist hospitals to treat infectious diseases and mental illness in the London area.[101] After 1867, the term 'state hospitals' began to be used rather than 'poor law infirmaries'.

In the following decades, conditions in poor law infirmaries gradually improved, and even began to attract patients prepared to pay for their treatment. By 1911 they catered for 120,000 patients.[102]

Workhouses also housed many lunatics. They, however, were primarily catered for by county asylums, which remained under the control of Quarter Sessions in 1834, and which are discussed in Chapter 10. Justices of the Peace had to authorise admissions on application from union relieving officers. After 1845, union medical officers also had to sign applications. Many lunatics were shuffled between workhouses and asylums.

Provision for the emigration of the poor was made by the 1834 Act. The cost had to be borne by emigrants' home parishes. In 1836, 5,241 emigrants were funded, the majority from Norfolk and Suffolk.[103] Emigration was boosted by two Acts of Parliament. Firstly, in 1848, responsibility for financing pauper emigration was assigned to unions rather than parishes. Secondly, in 1850, unions were granted authority to send pauper children aged under sixteen overseas. Between the 1870s and 1920s, thousands of pauper children were sent to Canada.[104] That included 1,500 from Bristol alone.[105] Many went with the voluntary societies mentioned in Chapter 3. In the 1830s, the Poor Law Commission's short-lived Migration Agency also helped the unemployed in counties such as Norfolk and Bedfordshire to migrate to northern England to find work in the new factories, not always successfully.[106]

Throughout its existence, the workhouse cast its shadow over a large section of the labouring classes. In 1908, 1.6% of the population entered a workhouse at some stage during the year. The percentage seems small, but it does mean that many of the poor had some experience of workhouse life, even if it was only for a week or two. They knew what to expect if they had the misfortune to become indigent. The Poor Law Commission had done its work only too well. They had 'founded a system based not on physical cruelty, but on psychological deterrence, on shame and fear'.[107] For the increasingly respectable working class, that was intolerable.

The nineteenth century saw attitudes towards institutions gradually change.[108] They had previously been seen as a last resort and avoided if at all possible. That applied, of course, particularly to workhouses – but it also applied to hospitals and lunatic asylums. Institutions were seen as being for the poor; they offered nothing to the wealthy. However, increasing professionalisation, and advances in healthcare, meant that they were increasingly used by those who were not poor. The proportion of deaths occurring in institutions doubled between 1879 and 1909. The sick made increasing use of hospitals, imbeciles were increasingly confined to lunatic asylums, and the government was increasingly placing emphasis on need rather than deterrence. In 1861, workhouses provided around 50,000 beds for the poor. By 1911, there were 121,161.[109]

Crime

Another important institution for the history of the poor was the nineteenth-century prison and its predecessors, the county gaol and the House of Correction. Poverty and crime were closely inter-related. The great majority of those convicted of crime in previous centuries were poor. That was partly due to the fact that the gentry feared the poor, did not trust them, and criminalised their behaviour. Richard Oastler's 1836 accusation that the aim of the Poor Law Amendment Act was to punish poverty as a crime[110] condemned an attitude towards poverty that many Justices of the Peace and Assize judges had applied to their work for centuries. It was true that some poor frequently felt that stealing a loaf of bread was better than starving. As for poaching, that was simply taking back what had already been stolen from you by the gentry.[111] In eighteenth-century London, 32.3% of those charged with crime were servants, who could easily be forced into crime for the sake of survival at some point in their lives. In contrast, 2.7% were gentlemen.[112] If you were a man of substance, you were unlikely to be a criminal, and even if you were found out you were likely to have powerful friends who could protect you from punishment.

The government's attitude to crime has gradually changed over the centuries. In the medieval period, threats to the integrity of government came primarily from over-mighty subjects, not from the poor. Central government was therefore not particularly interested in controlling low-level crime. But in the sixteenth and seventeenth century, government and society seemed to be increasingly challenged by the poor. Disorder and criminal behaviour among them increasingly seemed to threaten not only the Crown, but also the aristocrats, the gentry, and the merchants. Parliament increasingly sought to protect property, to strengthen criminal law, and to control the poor. In the eighteenth century, the crimes for which capital punishment could be imposed rapidly increased. However, the 'bloody code', as it was known, was rarely enforced; in practice, the number of hangings carried out actually decreased in the same period. The law was usually applied with moderation. Much depended on the views of local Justices of the Peace, although the poor could and did apply pressure when they thought that justice had been outraged. The exercise of authority was much more complex than simplistic ideas about the ruling class enforcing the law might imply.[113]

Popular perceptions of crime, and of the appropriate punishments, have gradually changed over the centuries. Punishment was not seen as the prime aim of criminal law and of the judiciary; rather, the purpose of the legal system was to maintain social cohesion. The strict letter of the law was usually only applied when it was thought that deterrence was needed. While murder attracted the death penalty until the twentieth century, even serious assault in the seventeenth and eighteenth century was frequently seen as a matter which required arbitration, rather than punishment. It was not regarded as felonious. By contrast, poaching was increasingly seen (by the gentry) as a serious crime. Customary practices such as gathering firewood and gleaning, on which the poor relied, began to be seen as theft. Many workers customarily retained for themselves the waste and surplus material left over after manufacture. Weavers kept the thrums – the weft ends left on a loom after weaving. Sawyers took away bags of sawdust. Framework knitters gathered up waste yarn. Such practices were increasingly criminalised during the Industrial Revolution.

Meanwhile, the enclosure of open fields across most of the Midlands, the drainage of the Fens, and agricultural improvements such as the introduction of threshing machines, all impacted on the poor. So did the introduction of tolls on the new turnpikes, and the imposition of new forms of taxation. These all caused unrest, and crime. Arsonists burnt farmers' haystacks; smugglers threatened excise officers; poachers took what they thought was theirs.

Crime, however, was only committed by a relatively small number of people. The poor as a class were not guilty, despite middle-class perceptions. Indeed, the majority of victims of crime were poor, and had a vested interest in preventing crime. In the mid-nineteenth century, it began to be realised that the 'poor' were not solely responsible for crime. Nineteenth-century statistics suggest that deprivation as a cause of crime was losing its explanatory power. Until 1850, criminal statistics moved in inverse relationship to the trade cycle: crime went up when trade was bad, and down when it was good. In the late nineteenth century, that gradually ceased to be the case, although admittedly there was an upsurge in crime during the Great Depression.[114] White-collar crime began to attract attention, with the prosecution of people like George

Lockups like this one at Hilperton (Wiltshire) could be used to punish minor offences.

Hudson, the railway promoter and fraudster. The growth of industry, and its need for large-scale financing, created many opportunities for dubious financiers, and for thousands of ill-paid clerks who had access to their employers' funds.[115] That is beyond the scope of this book, but it may be pointed out that such activities could result in poverty for their victims, and indeed for their perpetrators if found out. In this context, there are extensive records of bankruptcy and insolvent debtors, considered in Chapter 9.

A variety of punishments were available to early modern judges. Felony was subject to the death penalty, although many felons were pardoned or had their sentences reduced. Hanging was a common punishment, but heretics could be burnt, those who refused to plead could be crushed to death, and traitors could be hung, drawn and quartered. Mutilation, whipping, and the pillory or stocks, were lesser punishments. Fines were commonly

Cruikshank's Fagin in the condemned Cell.

imposed in cases of assault, and for lesser offences. Many were pardoned on condition that they joined the army or the Royal Navy.

Until the nineteenth century, gaols were not seen as places of punishment. Rather, they housed suspects committed for trial, and those awaiting hanging or whipping. They also housed debtors, and those unable to pay fines. They were theoretically the responsibility of county sheriffs, although the office of gaoler was normally farmed out. The gaoler was frequently a law unto himself, and conditions in gaols were disgraceful. John Howard's campaigns in the late eighteenth century presaged gradual improvements, and increased involvement from Quarter Sessions.

Punishment could, however, take place in Houses of Correction. These were first erected in accordance with Acts of 1576 and 1598; Justices were required to build them by the Vagabonds Act 1609. In conception, they were intended to provide work for the unemployed. In practice, unlike gaols, they were completely under the control of Quarter Sessions, and Justices of the Peace found a multitude of uses for them. Disobedient servants, apprentices, the workshy, and the mothers of illegitimate children, could all be incarcerated and put to work. Houses of Correction served as infirmaries for the sick, places of restraint for those with mental illnesses, and gaols for those suspected of felony or unable to pay fines. Inmates were provided with tools, and with raw materials such as wool, hemp, or flax, which they could work on. Salaried masters enforced strict work discipline (which could not be enforced in gaols). Many were built next to, or in conjunction with, prisons.

After 1708, judges made increasing use of the Houses of Correction to sentence convicted felons to hard labour.[116] That was curtailed after 1718, when it became possible to transport them to North America. When the United States declared independence in 1776, transportation temporarily ceased to be possible. Instead, many convicts served their sentences on prison hulks moored in the Thames. That continued even after the First Fleet sailed to Australia in 1788. Lesser offences continued to attract fines or a whipping, although these were increasingly carried out in private, rather than in the street. Incidentally, and strictly speaking, only those sentenced to hard labour, or to transportation, were described as convicts. Other offenders were prisoners, not convicts.[117]

In the mid-nineteenth century, sentencing practices gradually changed. The Australian colonies became increasingly less willing to accept convicts, and sentences of transportation gradually diminished. Transportation was replaced by incarceration in prison, perhaps with hard labour. Prison sentences also replaced whippings and the stocks for

The Convict Hulk Discovery at Deptford.

lesser offences, although fines continued to be imposed. Millbank Prison opened in 1816, Pentonville in 1842. Local responsibilities for gaols were gradually whittled away, and in 1877 the Home Office assumed total responsibility for the prison system. Houses of Correction had already been merged with the prison system in 1865. Consequently, many

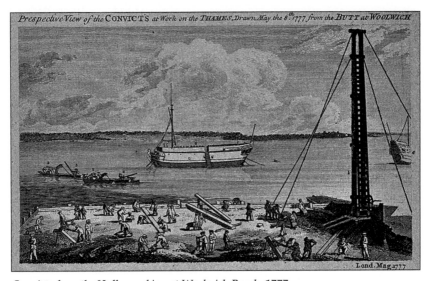

Convicts from the Hulks working at Woolwich Reach, 1777.

nineteenth- and twentieth-century registers of prisoners and similar documents are now in the National Archives.

Many of those charged with criminal offences were young. Whenever a major war ended, as in 1748, 1763 and 1783, there was an immediate increase in committals for theft. The youth who had been recruited as soldiers returned home without a livelihood, and consequently thievery surged. Youth crime continued to be a major problem into the twentieth century. Many of our criminal ancestors may have been in their teens and early twenties.

Charities

The prison and the workhouse both played important roles in the history of the poor. So did charities. Charities frequently worked in close collaboration with overseers and Guardians.[118] Indeed, they probably made greater provision for the poor than the Unions.[119] Many ran substantial institutions. Voluntary hospitals, orphanages, schools, and other institutions frequently pioneered new methods of care for the poor. For example, Great Ormond Street, England's first hospital for children, was founded in 1852. By 1888 there were thirty-eight children's hospitals in operation.[120] It is likely that the innumerable local organisations were even more important: mothers' meetings, Bible societies, sick benefit clubs, ragged schools, sewing classes. Many were devoted to visiting the poor; Prochaska has argued that, of the many forms of local benevolence provided, district visiting was the most important.[121] The Metropolitan Visiting and Relief Association was a federation of parish visiting societies.[122] The poor, however, sometimes found their status-conscious visitors patronising and over-bearing. Many set strict criteria for providing assistance; they were only interested in the 'respectable' poor, who were prepared to accept their rules. Those who could or would not do so were left to the tender mercies of the poor law authorities. The Charity Organisation Society acquired a reputation for pedantic meanness. A different approach was taken by the Ranyard Mission, which employed 'Bible women' to visit the poor. These missionaries-cum-social workers were working-class women drawn from the neighbourhood which they were to visit, and bridged the divide between the upper classes and the poor.[123] They laid the foundation of professional social work.

Many charities were formed to provide homes for destitute children, the sick, unmarried mothers, and the elderly. Some worked closely with poor law authorities; for example, the Metropolitan Association for Befriending Young Servants (see below, p.66) was established on the initiative of the first female poor law inspector. Voluntary hospitals led advances in medicine, and provided medical education. Faith in the ability of institutions to deal with social problems was widespread at the opening of the twentieth century.

The Welfare State

The early twentieth century saw the gradual formation of the welfare state. Free school meals for poor children, administered by local authorities rather than by Guardians, were introduced in 1906. Old-age pensions were introduced in 1908,[124] radically reducing the need for workhouses. In 1911, a national insurance scheme paying unemployment benefits was established. Although the number of residents in workhouses reached an all-time high of 280,000 in 1912, numbers declined thereafter, primarily owing to the new benefits.[125] From 1913, workhouses became 'poor law institutions', reflecting the fact that they no longer catered for the able-bodied poor. By 1920, the elderly, vagrants, and unmarried mothers formed the vast majority of inmates.[126] Nevertheless, the settlement laws remained in operation. In 1907 over 12,000 paupers were removed from one union to another.[127] It was not until 1948 that the settlement laws were finally removed from the statute book.

The Pauper Memorial at West Bromwich.

The 'new' poor law gradually lost its *raison d'être*, and Boards of Guardians were dissolved in 1930. Unemployment Assistance Committees took over the administration of outdoor relief. The

Poplar and Stepney Sick Asylum. Courtesy Wellcome Collection.

institutions they ran became known as 'public assistance institutions'. Workhouses and related institutions such as infirmaries became the responsibility of county councils. Many former union infirmaries became National Health Service hospitals; their records are likely to be listed by the Hospital Records Database **www.nationalarchives.gov.uk/ hospitalrecords**.[128] The National Assistance Act 1948 brought to an end the last vestiges of the 1834 Act.

Records of the Poor

The strategies of the poor which are best documented relate to charity, the poor law, and crime. This documentation, dating from the sixteenth century onwards, provides us with most of the sources we need to trace our poor ancestors, and these topics form the core of this book.

The records of the poor law, found principally among the archives of parishes and Quarter Sessions, are the most important sources for tracing poor ancestors. Official records provide us with many names of paupers. Documents such as settlement examinations and paupers' letters provide much interesting personal information. Accounts reveal how much relief was paid, and may record the nature of the payment.

Charities also created and retained many records, for example, apprenticeship indentures for the boys whose premiums they had paid. Much information on the poor, and especially on criminals, can be found in the archives of Quarter Sessions and Assizes.

Local record offices hold a vast amount of documentation arising from these sources. Further documentation can be found in the National Archives, for example: hearth tax exemption certificates, bankruptcy records and some criminal records. From the late eighteenth century, newspapers also provide valuable information, for example, advertisements for parish apprentices who had absconded, details of petitions for bankruptcy, accounts of criminal trials.

The poor are also frequently mentioned in documents of a more general nature, such as parish registers,[129] the census,[130] and the civil registers. These are mostly outside the scope of this book, although a couple of points relating to the way in which the poor are recorded in parish registers and the census are mentioned in Chapter 10.

Further reading

There are numerous works on the poor. Most deal with specific topics, and many are noted in the appropriate chapters below. A full listing of relevant works would occupy much more space than is available here. For nineteenth-century poverty, a useful listing is included in:

- Englander, David. *Poverty and Poor Law Reform in 19th century Britain, 1834–1914: from Chadwick to Booth.* Longman, 1998.

Many useful essays are included in:

- Hitchcock, Tim, King, Peter, & Sharpe, Pamela, eds. *Chronicling Poverty: the Voices and Strategies of the English Poor, 1640–1840.* Macmillan Press, 1997.

For a study of the inter-relationship between poor law officers and charity in Manchester, see:

- Hindle, G.B. *Provision for the Relief of the Poor in Manchester 1754–1826.* Chetham Society 3rd series 22. 1975.

A detailed study of the poor in London (accompanied by an extensive website) is provided by:

- Hitchcock, Tim, & Shoemaker, Robert. *London Lives: Poverty, Crime and the Making of a Modern City. 1690–1800.* Cambridge University Press, 2015. **www.londonlives.org**

There are a number of classic accounts of the state of the poor in the eighteenth and nineteenth century:[131]

- Eden, Frederick Morton. *The state of the poor* ... 3 vols. B. & J. White, 1797. Reprinted Bristol: Thoemmes, 1994. Eden includes some names; for example, he has an extensive 'Account of payments by the Overseer of the Poor of the parish of Bradford Wiltshire', made over thirteen weeks in 1792, listing recipients.[132]
- Mayhew, Henry. *London Labour and the London poor.* Griffin Bone & Co. 1861. There are various modern editions.
- Engels, Frederick. *The Condition of the working class in England in 1844, with appendix written 1886, and preface 1887.* New York: John W. Lovell, 1887. There are various modern editions.
- Booth, Charles. *Life and Labour of the People in London.* 17 vols. Macmillan, 1889–1902. Names from Booth's investigations are omitted from these volumes, but detailed case histories of both inmates and recipients of outdoor relief in 1888–9 are recorded in manuscript volumes held by the London School of Economics.[133] See Charles Booth's London: Stepney Union Casebooks **https://booth.lse.ac.uk/notebooks/stepney-union-casebooks**

Many contemporary writings on the poor law have been brought together in:

- Rose, Michael E. *The English Poor Law 1780–1930*. David & Charles, 1971.

A useful guide to the records of the poor is provided by:

- Burlison, Robert. *Tracing Your Pauper Ancestors: A Guide for Family Historians*. Pen & Sword, 2009.

See also:

- Fowler, Simon. *Poor law records for family historians*. Family History Partnership, 2011.
- Cole, Anne. *Poor law documents before 1834*. 2nd ed. Federation of Family History Societies, 2000.

Useful guidance to internet and other sources is provided by:

- Connected Histories: Poverty and poor relief: a research guide
  www.connectedhistories.org/guide.aspx?a=7

Many facsimiles of poor law documents are printed in:

- Hawkings, David T. *Pauper Ancestors: A Guide to the Records Created by the Poor Laws in England and Wales*. History Press, 2011.

Chapter 3

CHARITIES

Introduction

The church has always encouraged charitable giving. Indeed, the perceived need to regulate bequests given for pious purposes led the church to develop the great network of probate courts which lasted from medieval times until 1858, and the archives of which include the vast number of wills and probate inventories that family historians depend upon.[1] By the thirteenth and fourteenth century, almost 700 'hospitals' had been founded. The term 'hospital' originally referred to a place of hospitality. Some medieval hospitals did provide care for the diseased, but the term also encompassed almshouses and lodgings for travellers.[2]

Prior to the seventeenth century, most charities were founded by individual donors, frequently by bequests. Early philanthropists frequently founded institutions such as schools, almshouses, workhouses, orphanages, and hospitals. Some charities combined two or three of these functions.[3] Christ's Hospital in London, for example, was an orphanage with a school, rather than a hospital in the modern sense.

The eighteenth century has been described as the 'age of benevolence'.[4] It witnessed the development of the idea of association as the means of philanthropy. Charities began to be funded by public subscription, rather than by endowment. Charitable societies sprang up to administer the work. Many of the schools for the poor founded under the auspices of the SPCK were supported by subscription.[5] The first major public institution to use this method of funding was the Foundling Hospital, founded in 1739.

Changing needs caused philanthropists to direct their wealth to a variety of different purposes. From the sixteenth century onwards, the emphasis placed on apprenticeship led many donors to concentrate on paying the premiums needed to apprentice poor children. In the eighteenth and nineteenth century, before the state assumed responsibility for the education of the poor, schooling – and especially elementary education – was frequently provided by charities. So were orphanages. At the same time, the perceived desirability of sending paupers and other poor to settle in the colonies led to the creation of charities which would pay for their passage. Religious denominations ranging from the Salvation Army to the Roman Catholic Church were deeply involved in social work of various kinds.

Philanthropic endowments for the poor tended to favour institutions such as schools, hospitals, and orphanages, rather than the direct provision of relief in cash.[6] That, of course, was not always the case; Tewkesbury's Geast Charity, for example, regularly provided cash doles.[7] Philanthropists also tended to favour the 'deserving poor', rather than the most needy.[8] The extremity of some people's poverty disqualified them from receiving assistance from charities which discriminated against the 'undeserving'. The latter frequently included paupers. Even when a charity did try to help them, it could be thwarted. The Marine Society, which theoretically took vagrant boys off the streets to train them in seamanship, in practice found that ships' captains refused to accept such children. It consequently began to accept children from the families of 'deserving poor' who sought a cheap alternative to apprenticeship. Ill-thought-out provision could have dire consequences: parliamentary support for the Foundling Hospital in the mid-eighteenth century has been described as 'sparking the most expensive and murderous experiment in social welfare in British history', because it encouraged parents to abandon their children.

According to Fowler, the poor had a 'bewildering choice of charities from which to seek assistance'.[9] Consultation of directories is likely to yield details of a wide variety. Admittedly, charities tended to be concentrated in cathedral cities and market towns, rather than in the industrial centres of the north. And the rural poor were likely to find themselves dependent on the goodwill of the Anglican parish priest. Members of other denominations, such as the Quakers or the Methodists, might receive assistance from their co-religionists. Catholic priests were particularly noted for the assistance they gave to the poor. Church accounts sometimes record money given to the poor; for example, the Beverley Wesleyan Circuit account book lists sums given to poor members from 1868 to 1929.[10]

For centuries, charity dominated the provision of relief to the poor. It is difficult for the twenty-first-century mind to comprehend the importance of charity before the twentieth century. It was far more important than state provision of poor relief.[11] In the early 1860s, in London alone, it has been estimated that philanthropic activity (not just poor-related) raised between £5,500,000 and £7,000,000. Total poor law expenditure throughout England and Wales in 1861 totalled less than £6,000,000.[12] The development of the welfare state was very slow, and regarded with justifiable suspicion: jobbery, nepotism, corruption, and incompetence were rife in official circles, and it took many years for the general public to accept even the notion that central direction of poor relief was a good thing. It was not easy to persuade taxpayers that governmental administrative machinery could be relied on to be both efficient and honest. The electoral malpractices and party warfare which frequently marred elections for Boards of Guardians were hardly persuasive.[13] Many thought that the best method of solving social problems – if they were solvable – was to use private charity. The state could never do it: it was too impersonal, too bureaucratic, and too unwieldy. It lacked individual discretion. It has been estimated that, in the eighteenth century, between 20% and 30% of urban populations were reliant on charity, whereas only 4% to 8% were reliant on poor relief.[14]

It was not until the advent of the Welfare State that charity began to take a subordinate role in the provision of social welfare.[15] Even so, charitable institutions have not withered away as a consequence of the welfare state; quite the contrary. A 1943 survey identified 1,500 almshouse foundations accommodating over 22,000 people. By 1999, almshouses had space for 31,421 residents.[16]

Perry & Dawes Almshouse at Wootton under Edge.

The relationship between state welfare and charity has, however, always been cooperative, rather than competitive. Those who served local government, for example, as overseers, churchwardens, or guardians, frequently also acted as trustees of charities. Indeed, the foundation documents of many charities specified that local officials should act as trustees – although donors were sometimes careful to specify that funds should not be used to replace poor relief via the rates.[17] Local officials had an intimate knowledge of their localities, and could respond quickly and effectively to local needs. Their links to local government mean that their records can frequently be found among parish and borough records.

The charities themselves were not always well organised. There was much peculation, and many local charities were lost. One eighteenth-century commentator put forward two explanations for the disappearance of charity money: the cash 'has been lost, or embezzled by the Parish officers some time ago'.[18] The Charity Commission was established in 1853 to ensure that charitable funds were being used in accordance with the intentions of their founders. Charities could also be subjected to political criticism; the Charity Organisation Society, for example, thought that many were too indiscriminate in their alms-giving. Established in 1869, it aimed to coordinate charitable work, to encourage charities to interview applicants rigorously before granting assistance, and to establish local registers of the poor, working in close cooperation with Boards of Guardians.[19] Its initials were said by some to stand for 'Cringe or Starve'. Many charities refused to submit to its leadership, and it was much less important than its supporters liked to suggest,[20] but if any of its local registers can be found (perhaps among union records) they could provide useful information to genealogists. Its district visitors gathered information on all who asked for its aid, including details of their families, work, wages, health, and schooling.[21]

The philanthropic tradition continued into the twentieth century, despite the burgeoning welfare state. Charities redirected their efforts to problems that the state was not adequately dealing with. Many were old established, but their numbers were rapidly growing. By 1988, there were 166,000 charities registered with the Charity Commissioners.[22] Changing needs meant that their focus frequently differed from that of their predecessors; nevertheless, many continued to be concerned with providing help to the poor and needy.

The names of charity beneficiaries are frequently mentioned in documents such as trustees' minutes, annual reports, accounts, and disbursement lists. These records may provide much information about individuals.

It is not possible here to identify more than a handful of the charities which supported the poor. One of them was Henry Smith's Charity, which was created by a wealthy and astute businessman from Wandsworth who, legend has it, wandered the countryside with his dog (and was consequently known as 'Dog Smith'), dressed as a beggar. When he died in 1628, he left £1,000, invested in land for the poor. Today, his charity is one of the largest grant-making charities in Britain. Down through the centuries, it has made grants in numerous different parishes throughout the country. Grants were made in association with parish officers. Papers relating to them, sometimes naming the poor who received alms, were frequently deposited in parish chests. Many are listed by the National Archives Discovery Catalogue **http://discovery.nationalarchives.gov. uk**. The charity has its own website:

- The Henry Smith Charity: History
  www.henrysmithcharity.org.uk/about-us/history

Many charities were of local rather than national importance. That applied to Tewkesbury's Charles Geast Charity, which distributed its income among the town's poor. A small number of its beneficiaries are listed in its very detailed accounts, which also identify its feoffees and other officers, and its many tenants.[23]

The 'hospital' endowed by Hugh Sexey at Bruton in the early seventeenth century was another charity that was important locally. Its almshouse could only accommodate twelve inmates, but it also provided casual 'gratuities' to many others, as well as paying premiums for poor apprentices. Unusually, its archives include many petitions for gratuities, as well as the more usual apprenticeship indentures.[24]

Charities were frequently administered by municipal and parish officers, and their records may survive among city and parish archives. In Oxford, disbursements made by municipal charities were meticulously recorded, and 494 pensioners of various charities are recorded in the corporation book of elections to charities, 1740–70.[25]

An attempt to compile a comprehensive description of every charity in England, on a county basis, was made by the Commissioners for Inquiring concerning Charities, and published by HMSO between 1819 and 1840. These reports can usually be found in local studies libraries and record offices. *Digests of endowed charities* were regularly published among the Parliamentary papers (see p.5–6) from 1867 onwards. From 1882, *The Charities Register and Digest*, published by the Charity Organisation Society, provided an annual listing of contemporary charities. For addresses of charities which still exist, visit:

- Search the Charity Register database
  www.gov.uk/find-charity-information

Nineteenth-century charities based in London are listed in:
- Low, Sampson. *The Charities of London in 1861, comprising an account of the operations, resources and general condition of the Charitable, Educational, and Religious Institutions of London.* Sampson Low, Son & Co., 1862.

Much useful information on charities based in Bloomsbury (both local and national), including details of available archives, is provided by:

- UCL Bloomsbury Project: Institutions
  www.ucl.ac.uk/bloomsbury-project/institutions/

For a detailed historical survey of English philanthropy, see:

- Owen, David. *English Philanthropy, 1660–1960.* Harvard University Press, 1965.

Briefer introductions include:

- Alvey, Norman. *From Chantry to Oxfam: a short history of charity and charity legislation.* British Association for Local History, 1995.
- Prochaska, Frank. *The Voluntary Impulse: philanthropy in Modern Britain.* Faber & Faber, 1988.

Almshouses

Almshouses are among the oldest charitable institutions. Holy Cross Hospital at Winchester, for example, was founded in 1136 to accommodate thirteen 'impotent' almsmen, and to provide food to another hundred indigent poor 'of good conduct'.[26] The number of almshouses, however, was always small. Approximately 87.25% of parishes never had a dedicated almshouse, and the proportion of the elderly living in almshouses has never been higher than 2.9%.[27] In Dorset, for example, only just over forty almshouses are known to have existed.[28] From the eighteenth century, their contribution became even more limited as the social background of beneficiaries narrowed – although it is probably true that almshouses have always catered for the 'respectable poor'.[29] In nineteenth-century Sherborne, many almsmen were agricultural labourers, while many almswomen were laundresses. Other trades

Jesus Hospital, Bray.

included cordwainers, tailors, carpenters, and stone masons. Some almswomen had been silk workers. A few almsmen had been masters in their trades.[30]

The residents of almshouses were not looked down on in the same way as the residents of union workhouses in the nineteenth century. Almsmen had to fulfil the requirements for admittance laid down in foundation statutes, and they had to obey regulations governing their conduct.

The earliest occupants of almshouses are not very well documented. For example, most records of the sixteenth-century St John's Hospital at Winchester date from after 1829. Surviving records identifying almsmen are rare before the nineteenth century, although they do exist. In Surrey, 121 almshouses have been identified, but only nine kept registers.[31] The almsmen of Christchurch Almshouse in Oxford can be identified in the Patents which recorded their admissions, in disbursement books, and in other almshouse archives.[32] It is fairly rare to find a document such as the extensive list of admissions found in the Sherborne Almshouse register.[33] This identifies hundreds of almsmen, 1582–1866, and also includes a variety of other documents.

Almshouse at Ross on Wye.

If the records of trustees are not to be found, other sources may yield information. The earliest list of almsmen accommodated by the Leamington Hastings Almshouse is found in a 1634 petition to Chancery. Some of the names on it can be linked to entries in the parish register. At a later date, burial entries in the register, and entries in overseers' accounts relating to burials in woollen, occasionally identify a 'beadswoman', or 'a member of the Hospitall'.[34] Where overseers were trustees, their accounts may name the almsmen to whom they gave assistance.

Later records are more likely to survive. For example, a register of the inmates of Sowerby Almshouse, 1854–1993, which also includes trustees' minutes and accounts, is held by West Yorkshire Archive Service. Bristol Archives holds late nineteenth- and early twentieth-century records of Lady Haberfield's Almshouse Trust, listing inmates according to the rooms in which they dwelt. There is also a list of petitions for out-pensions, 1909–17. Between 1841 and 1911, of course, almsmen can be identified in the decennial censuses.

For the history of almshouses from the point of view of inmates, see:

- Nicholls, Angela. *Almshouses in early modern England: charitable housing in the mixed economy of welfare.* Boydell Press, 2017.
- Goose, Nigel, et al., eds. *The British Almshouse: new perspectives on philanthropy.* FACHRS Publications, 2016.

A detailed account of the origins of medieval almshouses, together with a brief history of each institution in Devon and Cornwall, is provided by:

- Orme, Nicholas, & Webster, Margaret. *The English Hospital 1070–1570.* Yale University Press, 1995.

Many books on almshouses concentrate on their founders and their architecture, rather than their inmates. Such works may help to identify institutions where ancestors lived. See, for example:

- Bailey, Brian. *Almshouses.* Robert Hale, 1988.

Almshouses continue to operate even today. Details of historic almshouses are usually given in the parish histories published by the Victoria County History, most of which can be read at **www.british-history.ac.uk.**Some are listed at **www.workhouses.co.uk/almshouses**
A number of record societies have published almshouse records naming inmates. The Sherborne register has already been mentioned. See also, for example:

- Hitchcock, Timothy V., ed. *Richard Hutton's complaints book: the notebook of the steward of the Quaker Workhouse at Clerkenwell, 1711–1737.* London Record Society 24. 1987.
- Crowley, Douglas, ed. *The Minute Books of the Froxfield Almshouse, 1714–1866.* Wiltshire Record Society 66. 2013.
- Wordsworth, Chr., ed. *The Fifteenth century cartulary of St Nicholas' Hospital, Salisbury, with other records.* Wiltshire Record Society 3. 1902. The 'other records' includes a list of brethren and sisters down to 1899.

Apprentices

The practice of apprenticing young people began in twelfth- and thirteenth-century London. The apprentice would live in his master's household for seven years while he learnt his trade; the master would provide board, lodging, clothing, and instruction; the apprentice would work for his master while being taught. Both master and apprentice were expected to abide by their indentures, which both had signed, and which were sometimes recorded in borough registers. Initially, premiums were not expected, but the practice of paying them grew up in the fifteenth and sixteenth century. The higher the status of the trade, of course, the higher the premium, and the better the prospects of the apprentice.

The 1563 Statute of Artificers and Apprentices required everyone to be an apprentice, although the law was not always enforced. The poor were frequently not in a position to pay premiums for their children. Pauper children were forced to accept the austere conditions imposed by poor law overseers, who had the power to bind them apprentice without their parents' consent (see Chapter 4). Many, however, were removed from pauperism by apprenticeship charities, established by wealthy philanthropists. They bore the cost of premiums. Sometimes they provided other benefits, such as lump sums when apprentices completed their servitude.

Hugh Sexey's Hospital at Bruton (Somerset) has already been mentioned as a good example of a 'hospital' which regularly apprenticed poor boys.[35] Many similar charities can be identified in the Commissioners' reports mentioned above. These charities were frequently involved in other activities as well; for example, the Foundling Hospital (see below, p.55–7) brought their children up, sent them to school, and then apprenticed them. Many county charities established by the gentry, such as the Wiltshire Society,[36] were London dining clubs which supported apprenticeship. Local apprenticeship charities were frequently run by parish and borough officers. Trade guilds, such as Exeter's Incorporation of Weavers, Fullers and Shearmen,[37] sometimes ran apprenticeship charities. Similarly, the sons of poor burgesses in Gloucester benefited from a charity which paid their apprenticeship premiums.[38] These were the privileged poor, whose lot was much better than that of pauper apprentices.[39] (See below, p.55–7).

Indentures followed a standard format, which changed little over the centuries. Charity indentures are likely to provide the following information:

- The name of the apprentice and his parents or guardian(s), with the father's occupation and/or residence. Children were frequently apprenticed on the death of their fathers, so many indentures indicate that mothers are widows.
- The name of the master, his occupation and place of residence, and perhaps the name of his wife.
- The name of the charity and its trustees (many of whom were borough, parish, or guild officers)
- The trade which the apprentice will learn
- The amount of the premium
- The term to be served
- The names of witnesses

Other information may also be provided, for example, any provisions made for the apprentice at the end of his term, changes of master, or other variations to the terms of the indenture made during the apprenticeship.

Clarissa Harlowe, for example, changed masters so many times that no space could be found on the back of her indenture to enter details when she was turned over to yet another master in 1765.[40]

Charity indentures are most likely to be found among the records of the charity concerned. Independent charities sometimes deposited their records separately, but others may be found among parish and guild records, and in solicitors' archives. A few indentures have been digitised; for example, indentures from Plymouth's Orphan's Aid Educational Foundation (1868–1908) have been made available by Find My Past **www.findmypast.co.uk**.

Charity trustees retained one of the three copies of the indenture that were made. The other two copies were retained by the apprentice (or his father), and the master. These copies are less likely to survive.

In addition to the indentures, charities may have other records. Accounts recording the payment of premiums may give the names of both master and apprentice. In some instances, a payment was made to the apprentice on successful completion of his term, and that too may be recorded in the accounts. Some charities kept registers of the apprentices they indentured. These provide the researcher with abstracts of indentures, and may be useful if the indentures themselves have been lost. Many boroughs kept registers of private indentures, which sometimes include those prepared by charity trustees.

A detailed guide to apprenticeship records is provided by:

• Raymond, Stuart A. *My Ancestor was an Apprentice: how can I find out more about him?* Society of Genealogists Enterprises, 2010.

Education
The provision of education has always been a priority for the church. We will see below (p.55, 98-9, and 157) how provision for the education of the poor was made in sixteenth-century London, at Christ's Hospital, and at Bridewell, and how they provided the models for similar institutions. The growth of the charity school movement owed much to the work of the Society for the Promotion of Christian Knowledge (SPCK), which began its work to 'spread practical Christianity among the godless poor' in 1698.[41]

Although charity schools were intended to benefit the poor, that did not necessarily mean paupers. Occasionally pauper children were sent to them, and payments for schooling do appear in overseers' accounts. At least in eighteenth-century Oxford, however, the great majority of charity pupils were not receiving support from their parishes.[42] Children admitted to endowed schools were frequently required to secure nomination from subscribers. Pauper children were not regarded as being among the 'respectable poor', so only infrequently received such nominations.[43]

In the eighteenth and nineteenth century, many churches ran Sunday Schools for the education of children who had to work, and could not attend during the week. Many poor children learnt to read and write at such schools, which also aimed to provide a Christian education. The Ragged School movement, aimed at providing education to the most destitute children, began in the late eighteenth century. The Ragged Schools Union, founded in 1844, aimed to provide education, food, clothing and lodging to children who were unable to attend Sunday School due to their unkempt appearance and frequently challenging behaviour. Between 1844 and 1881, some 300,000 children were helped.

Ragged schools ceased to operate after 1870, when their work was taken over by the government's elementary Board schools. Registers and other records of ragged schools are sometimes held in local record offices. The National Archives also holds some records of ragged schools, in the ED classes, but not many of these name pupils. Useful information on ragged schools can be found at:

- Ragged University: Education History: A Brief History of Ragged Schools
  www.raggeduniversity.co.uk/2012/08/08/history-ragged-schools-2

Sunday schools also flourished in the nineteenth century. No less than 19% of the eligible population attended them in 1885. Sunday School records may be among the archives of the churches which ran them; these are likely to have been deposited in local record offices.

Beyond the Sunday schools, churches also sought to provide full-time elementary education for the poor. The Church of England, the Nonconformists, and the Roman Catholics, all ran societies devoted to this purpose. For the Anglicans, there was the National Society for Promoting the Education of the Poor in the Principles of the Established Church. The Nonconformists had the British and Foreign Schools Society. The Catholic Poor Schools Committee (renamed the Catholic Education Council in 1905) was particularly concerned for the spiritual well-being of the children of poor Irish immigrants.[44] These were all nineteenth-century institutions, but many of the schools supported by the first two had in fact been founded through subscriptions in the previous century, frequently as a result of the activities of the SPCK.[45] The Education Act 1870, which established the principle of free elementary education for all, was action by the state to supplement voluntary activity, certainly not to replace it.

Many educational charities retained extensive central archives. Those of the National Society are held by Lambeth Palace Library; see **www. lambethpalacelibrary.org/files/Education.pdf**. The British and Foreign Schools Society archives are held by Brunel University, and described by **www.bfss.org.uk/archive**. See also **www.brunel.ac.uk/about/Archives/ British-and-Foreign-School-Society-BFSS-Archive**. St Mary's University, Twickenham, holds the archives of the Catholic Poor Schools Committee, which are described by AIM25 **www.aim25.com**.

The family historian is most likely to be interested in the registers of pupils kept by individual schools, which have frequently been deposited in local record offices. Many have been digitised by Find My Past:

- National School Admission Registers & Log-Books 1870–1914
  https://search.findmypast.co.uk/search-world-records/national-school-admission-registers-and-log-books-1870-1914

There were a variety of other educational charities, some of which also ran schools. It is not possible to list them all here, but many registers are in print or online. See, for example:

- Simmonds, Mark John. *Register of the Clergy Orphan School of Boys, 1751–1896.* Augustine's College, 1897.
- Redhill Royal Philanthropic School Admission Registers 1788–1906
  www.findmypast.co.uk/articles/world-records/full-list-of-united-kingdom-records/institutions-and-organisations/redhill-royal-philanthropic-school-admission-registers-1788-1906
  School for homeless children.

Many records of charity schools remain unpublished, but can be consulted in local record offices. For example, the Northern Counties School for the Deaf was based in Newcastle upon Tyne. Its governors' minutes, accounts, log books and registers, 1838–1944, are held by Tyne and Wear Archives.

Further Reading
A detailed guide to the records of childhood, which includes extensive details of relevant archives and websites, is provided by:

- Wilkes, Sue. *Tracing your Ancestors' Childhood: a Guide for Family Historians.* Pen & Sword, 2013.

For a general introduction to educational records held by the National Archives, see:

- Elementary and primary schools
  www.nationalarchives.gov.uk/help-with-your-research/research-guides/elementary-primary-schools

School records outside of the National Archives are described by:

- Education history records held by other archives
  www.nationalarchives.gov.uk/help-with-your-research/research-guides/education-history-records-held-by-other-archives

For the eighteenth-century historical background, consult:

- Jones, M.G. *The Charity School Movement: a Study of Eighteenth-Century Puritanism in Action.* Cambridge University Press, 1938. Reprinted Frank Cass, 1964.

Orphanages and Children's Homes

Many charities have been devoted to the care of children. They have focused particularly on those who needed care – orphans and the destitute. In the past, the term 'orphan' was frequently applied to those who had only lost their fathers. There have been orphanages since at least Tudor times, but the late eighteenth century saw the foundation of many charitably funded orphanages or 'asylums', especially in London. Many were founded for the children of particular occupations. For example, from 1712 Greenwich Royal Hospital took in the orphans of mariners. The Clergy Orphan Society catered for the orphans of clergymen from 1749. The Metropolitan Police opened an orphanage at Twickenham for police orphans in 1871. The Railway Servants' Orphanage was opened in Derby in 1874. Other categories were also catered for. Both the Marine Society, and Shaftesbury Homes, searched out orphans and the destitute poor to train as seamen. Founded in 1865, the National Industrial Home for Crippled Boys provided for 'destitute, neglected, or ill-used cripples' aged between thirteen and eighteen. Various Christian denominations founded institutions for their co-religionists. The Roman Catholics were particularly active; they wanted to ensure that their destitute and orphaned children – of whom there were many – were nurtured in their own faith. Only a Catholic institution could protect them from anti-Catholic prejudice and hostility, and from Protestant proselytising. Many Catholic dioceses established rescue societies. Catholic orders such as the Daughters of Charity of St Vincent de Paul established many orphanages.

By the late nineteenth century, institutional care was widely available. Some societies ran numerous orphanages throughout England and Wales; several of these are discussed below. Others were much smaller, with only a few homes. James Fegan, for example, founded several orphanages in London and the south-east. Charles Haddon Spurgeon, the well-known Baptist preacher, who sought to imitate Müller's work in Bristol (see below, p.59), founded an orphans' home for boys in Stockwell, south London. Children's societies frequently saw emigration as a viable alternative to residential care, and many ran emigration schemes.

The children of paupers, of course, were the responsibility of Poor Law Guardians after 1834. Mostly, they were placed in workhouses, but some unions sent their children to homes run by charities. From the 1850s, children who had committed criminal offences were placed in reformatory schools. These gave way in the 1930s to approved schools.

In the twentieth century, there was a gradual move away from the large monolithic institution to supposedly more child-friendly 'cottage homes'. The practice of fostering reduced the pressure on places in institutions; indeed, after 1946 it became the preferred option. Formal adoption (see Chapter 10) also became increasingly popular. In 1955, the Foundling Hospital ceased to provide residential care for children, and switched its concern to other child-related activities.[46] In the following decades, most other children's charities followed suit. Local authorities became the front-line provider of services for children in need. By 1987, the number of children in residential homes had been reduced to 14,000.

A general history of orphanages in provided by:

- Higginbotham, Peter. *Children's Homes: A History of Institutional Care for Britain's Young.* Pen & Sword, 2017.

Useful websites include:

- Childrens' Homes: the Institutions that became Home for Britain's Children and Young People
  www.childrenshomes.org.uk
- Former Children's Homes
  www.formerchildrenshomes.org.uk

A variety of records were kept by children's homes. Case files and admission/discharge registers are likely to be particularly useful. You may also find annual reports, committee minutes, correspondence and other documents, all of which may provide useful information. In order to trace these records, you need first to identify the institution you are interested in. A number of works listing charities have already been mentioned; these should be checked. Consultation of local trade directories, Ordnance Survey maps, and/or the decennial census may also yield information. Once the name of the institution has been established, it can be searched for in the union catalogues mentioned above, p.3. Be aware, however, that the records of many smaller children's homes have been lost. Catholic institutions, especially those run by dioceses, have frequently deposited their records with Catholic diocesan archives, but there is no central list.[47] Commercial database hosts have digitised a few orphanage records; for example Ancestry **www.ancestry.co.uk** holds a list of children accommodated by the Royal Female Orphanage at Beddington (Surrey), between 1890 and 1913. Find My Past **www.findmypast.co.uk** has the register of the Derby Railway Servants' Orphanage 1875–1912. The successors of several of the larger institutions, most of which have ceased to provide homes, retain their own records. Understandably, they tend to keep strict control over access to personal records, especially relatively recent records.

Many nineteenth- and twentieth-century records relating to governmental policy and administration, including, for example, inspection reports, are held by The National Archives. These rarely include children's names. However, it may be useful to consult them for background information, although some registers of reformatory schools are held in HO 349. For details of children's home records at the National Archives, see:

- How to look for records of ... Children's Homes
  www.nationalarchives.gov.uk/help-with-your-research/research-guides/children-care/#5-childrens-homes-1834-1930

A detailed guide to tracing orphanage records is provided by:

- Limbrick, Gudrun Jane. *How to Research Childhoods spent in former children's homes, orphanages, cottage homes and other children's institutions.* Wordworks, 2013.

The records of some of the major institutions demand separate notice. A few have retained their own records, which they may make available to enquirers. Others have deposited them in record offices. Either way, strict control is generally maintained over access to more recent records.

Barnardo's

The name Barnardo's became almost synonymous with childrens' homes in the late nineteenth and early twentieth century. Dr Barnardo was a member of the Plymouth Brethren who intended to take up missionary work in China after he completed his training as a doctor. However, his encounters with destitute and homeless children in London led him to take a different direction. He began his work in Stepney in 1868, opening his first home for boys in 1870. The number of children in his care steadily increased; by his death in 1905 there were homes throughout the country, and an emigration scheme had been established. This work continued until after the Second World War, but in the late twentieth century the homes slowly closed as Barnardo's work with children went in new directions. The last home closed in 1989.

Barnardo's still has extensive records of the children who were in its care. Its Family History Service will search these records for you. Details of this service, together with an account of Barnardo's history, and a directory of former homes, can be found at

- Barnardos: Our History
  www.barnardos.org.uk/who-we-are/our-history

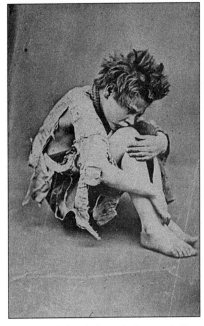

Dr. Barnardo.

A Barnardo boy before admittance to the Home.

Catholic Children's Society (formerly Crusade of Rescue)
This society retains records relating to its children's homes, child migrants, and Catholic workhouse children. For details of access, visit:

- Catholic Childrens Society: Pathways: Post Adoption and Aftercare
  www.cathchild.org.uk/pathways

Christ's Hospital
One of the earliest orphanages was Christ's Hospital in London, founded by Edward VI. It provided food, clothing, lodging and 'a little learning for fatherless children and other poor men's children'. It began with 380 children. Those who were too young for school were put out to nurse in Essex and Hertfordshire. Children wore blue coats; hence it was known as the Blue Coat School. It formed the model for many other 'blue coat' schools throughout the country (whose archives are frequently to be found in local record offices). However, like them, Christ's Hospital gradually became 'gentrified', and ceased to care for the poor. Foundlings were an early victim of this process; technically, a child left at its gates was within the parish of Christ Church, and therefore the parish was liable for any claims to poor relief on its behalf. Consequently, from 1676, foundlings ceased to be admitted.[48] Christ's Hospital eventually developed into an independent boarding school, moving to Horsham in 1902.

The archives are held by London Metropolitan Archives, although it also has its own museum **www.chmuseum.org.uk**. Admission registers are complete from 1563 to the late 1990s; minutes of the governors from 1556 to 1990 are also available for consultation. For further information visit:

- Records of Christ's Hospital and Bluecoat Schools
  www.cityoflondon.gov.uk/things-to-do/london-metropolitan-archives/visitor-information/Documents/29-records-of-christs-hospital-and-bluecoat-schools.pdf

Foundling Hospital
Thomas Coram established the Foundling Hospital in 1749, two centuries after Christ's Hospital. The name of the Foundling Hospital is a misnomer; most of its children were placed with the institution by their mothers, and records were kept. The governors thus evaded the fact that unknown children placed at its doors would automatically be regarded as settled in the local parish, and thus eligible for relief from local parish overseers. That problem had defeated a number of previous attempts to

The Foundling Hospital.

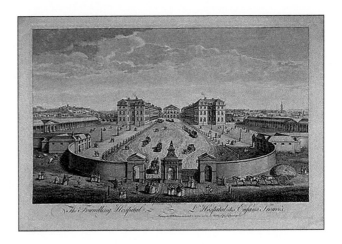

institutionalise the care of Foundlings.[49] Only babies under two months old were admitted. They were renamed and placed with wet nurses in the country until they were aged four or five, then they came back to London for schooling. Girls were apprenticed as servants for four years at the age of sixteen; boys were apprenticed to a trade for seven years at age fourteen. The Hospital as a residential institution was closed down in 1955.

The archives of the Foundling Hospital are now held by London Metropolitan Archives. Each child is extensively documented. The general registers give the date of admission, the child's number, child's (new) name, the date sent to nurse, and the date of apprenticeship, discharge or death. Admission books add the name of the petitioner (usually the mother), together with the nurse's name and residence. Billet books contain the token which mothers had to give so that they could identify their babies if their circumstances changed and they wished to reclaim them. Apprenticeship registers record details of apprenticeships. Some children were reclaimed by their mothers. Mothers' petitions claiming children, 1758–96, survive. Perhaps most importantly for family historians, after 1763 mothers seeking to place their babies in the Hospital had to submit petitions explaining their circumstances, and why they could not look after their children. These petitions may also identify the father. The testimonials provided by masters when apprentices completed their term may also be very useful. On receipt of the testimonial, the Hospital provided the apprentice with funds to advance their careers.

For a detailed guide to the records, including a useful bibliography, see:

- Finding your Foundling: A guide to finding records in the Foundling Hospital Archives
www.cityoflondon.gov.uk/things-to-do/london-metropolitan-archives/visitor-information/Documents/33-finding-your-foundling.pdf

See also:

- The Foundling Hospital Records
www.cityoflondon.gov.uk/things-to-do/london-metropolitan-archives/the-collections/Pages/foundling-hospital-records.aspx

The Hospital has its own museum:

- Foundling Museum
www.coram.org.uk/foundling-museum

Many histories are available; the most useful are probably:

- Pugh, Gillian. *London's Forgotten Children: Thomas Coram and the Foundling Hospital.* Tempus, 2007.
- McClure, Ruth. *Coram's Children: The London Foundling Hospital in the Eighteenth Century.* Yale University Press, 1981.

Gillian Clark has edited a collection of Foundling Hospital letters dealing with its practice of placing children with wet nurses. A detailed introduction is included in:

- Clark, Gillian, ed. *Correspondence of the Foundling Hospital Inspectors in Berkshire 1757–1768.* Berkshire Record Society, 1. 1994. Online at **www.berkshirerecordsociety.org.uk**

Petitions to the Foundling Hospital, and a variety of other documents, are edited in:

- Levene, Alysa, ed. *Narratives of the Poor in Eighteenth-Century Britain, volume 3: Institutional Responses: the London Foundling Hospital.* Pickering & Chatto, 2006.

Marine Society

The Marine Society **www.marine-society.org/history** was founded in 1756 to recruit and train orphans and other boys from poor backgrounds for naval service. Its founder, Jonas Hanway, also became a trustee of the Foundling Hospital. Many boys were trained in on-shore establishments, but in 1786 the Society acquired one of the earliest training ships. Boys typically joined the ships at age eleven or twelve, and stayed until they were fifteen or sixteen. Between 1756 and 1940, over 110,000 men and boys became seamen as a result of the Society's work.

The Society's archives are held at the National Maritime Museum's Caird Library. They include minutes, registers and accounts, 1756 to 1978. Registers cover:

- boys admitted, 1756 to 1763 and 1889 to 1958
- boys received and discharged from the Society's ship, 1786 to 1874
- boys entered as servants in the King's ships, 1770 to 1873
- apprentices sent to merchant ships, 1772 to 1950
- girl apprentices, 1772 to 1957.

For a full description of the archives, visit:

- Royal Museums Greenwich: Archive Catalogue: Marine Society
  https://collections.rmg.co.uk/archive/objects/492005.html

The Marine Society.

Müller's Orphan Homes

George Müller began working with destitute and homeless children in Bristol in 1836. Between then and 1958, his homes cared for over 17,000 orphans, although they never expanded to other parts of the country. Records of the orphans are still held by the institution; there is also a museum. For details, visit:

- Müller's
  www.mullers.org

National Children's Home

Thomas Bowman Stephenson was a Methodist minister when he encountered homeless children in Lambeth. His response was much the same as Barnardo's. A home for them was opened in 1869. It moved to Bethnal Green when the Methodist Conference moved Stephenson to that Circuit in 1871. An emigration scheme was established in 1873, and a home opened in Hamilton, Ontario. Expansion in England followed when a seventy-acre estate at Edgworth, Lancashire, was donated. Expansion continued throughout the rest of the nineteenth century and into the twentieth. The name National Children's Home was adopted in 1908, and it became one of the largest children's charities in the UK. The shift of focus away from the provision of residential care was marked when the name was changed to NCH Action for Children in 1994, and shortened to Action for Children in 2008. Records of children formerly in the care of the NCH are still held by the charity; they may include admission forms detailing the reasons for admission, information regarding birth relatives, birth certificates, school reports, and other documents. For access details, visit:

- Action for Children
  www.actionforchildren.org.uk
  Click 'What we Do' and 'Help if you were formerly in our care'

Advert for the National Children's Home. (Courtesy Wellcome Collection)

Shaftesbury Homes and Arethusa

The history of this organisation began with the founding of a ragged school in Holborn in 1843. A 'refuge' for homeless children was opened in 1852. The work attracted the patronage of Lord Shaftesbury, who arranged for redundant warships to be made available for training boys in seamanship. A number of other orphanages were also conducted by this institution. Its archives are held by London Metropolitan Archives. See also:

- The Shaftesbury Homes and Arethusa
  www.childrenshomes.org.uk/SH

Waifs and Strays Society

In 1881, this society was founded by Edward de Montjoie Rudolf, a Church of England Sunday school teacher in south Lambeth, who objected to the non-denominational approach taken by Dr Barnardo. He aimed to provide homes for destitute homeless children. By 1905, the Society had 3,410 children in its care, with ninety-three homes scattered throughout England and Wales. Perhaps a quarter of the children were fostered. Between 1887 and 1914, 2,250 children were sent to Canada. In 1946, the Society changed its name to the Church of England Children's Society, and since 1982 it has been known as the Children's Society. It no longer runs orphanages.

The Society maintains its own archives, which primarily consist of 140,000 case files for individual children assisted by the Society. These archives are catalogued at **www.calmview.eu/childrensociety/Calmview**.

A brief history of the Society, including some anonymised examples of files, is available at:

- Hidden Lives Revealed: a Virtual Archive: Children in Care 1881–1981
  www.hiddenlives.org.uk/cases/

See also:

- The Waifs & Strays Story
  www.childrenshomes.org.uk/WS

Emigration

Between the seventeenth and twentieth century, emigration was frequently sponsored by poor law authorities. In the nineteenth century charities began to do so too. We have already seen that children's homes frequently ran emigration schemes. There were also a number of charitable organisations focused on sending children overseas. One of the earliest initiatives was made by the Petworth Emigration Committee in the 1830s. It sent numerous emigrants from Sussex and adjacent counties to Canada. For details of its activities, and a detailed biographical listing of the emigrants it sponsored, see:

- Cameron, Wendy, & Maude, Mary McDougall. *Assisting emigration to Upper Canada: The Petworth Project 1832–1837.* McGill-Queens University Press, 2000.

Child emigration increased rapidly from the 1860s, due to the work of Maria Rye and Annie Macpherson, who independently began organising the resettlement of children in Canada. In 1870, Father Nugent accompanied twenty-four Catholic children to Canada; in the following decades many followed. Barnardo's was another major charity involved in emigration. It worked closely with Poor Law Guardians, but found itself with a problem when the Wellington Guardians, in 1913, asked them for help with Mary Ann Warren. Barnardo's sent her to Canada, but she was returned due to ill health; there are many letters relating to the case in the Wellington Union's archives.[50]

A useful (if admittedly dated) factsheet on child migrants, produced by the Department of Health, which lists many other sending organisations, is provided by:

- Former British Child Migrants
  http://webarchive.nationalarchives.gov.uk/20100415223817/http://www.dh.gov.uk/prod_consum_dh/groups/dh_digitalassets/@dh/@en/documents/digitalasset/dh_4090030.pdf

Between 1870 and 1940, perhaps 100,000 child emigrants, often known as 'British Home Children', were sent to Canada by a variety of sending organisations. Many of these children are listed by the British Home Children Registry. This database, together with much other useful information, is available at:

- British Home Children in Canada
  http://canadianbritishhomechildren.weebly.com

For a guide to records held by Library and Archives Canada, see:

• Home Children 1869–1932
  **www.bac-lac.gc.ca/eng/discover/immigration/immigration-records/
  home-children-1869-1930/Pages/home-children.aspx**

For Catholic children sent to Canada, visit:

• Library and Archives Canada: Catholic Organizations
  **www.bac-lac.gc.ca/eng/discover/immigration/immigration-records/
  home-children-1869-1930/home-children-guide/Pages/catholic-
  organizations.aspx**

The Children's Friend Society, established in 1830, sent its first children to Australia in 1832. It was not, however, until the twentieth century that large numbers of children were being sent 'down under'. The main agencies were the Fairbridge Society, the Dreadnought Trust, and the Big Brother Movement. After 1923, they received financial assistance from the British government. For a detailed account of their history, and a useful guide to archives available in Australia, see:

• Coldrey, Brian. *Good British Stock: Child and Youth Migration to Australia.* National Archives of Australia, 1999. Digitised at **http://guides.naa. gov.au/good-british-stock/**

Fairbridge Society archives are described by:

• Fairbridge Society, Records [United Kingdom] (1908 - c. 2007)
  www.findandconnect.gov.au/ref/wa/biogs/WE00829b.htm

The Christian Brothers were a smaller group. For details of the Christian Brothers Ex-Residents and Students Services Personal History Index, visit **www.cbers.org/archive/phind.asp.htm**.

Further Reading
For the historical background to child migration, see:

• Kershaw, Roger, & Sacks, Janet. *New lives for old.* National Archives, 2008.

For an interesting history of pauper and other poor children sent to Canada, see:

- Parker, Roy. *Uprooted: the shipment of poor children to Canada 1867–1917*. Policy Press, 2010.

See also:

- Parr, Joy. *Labouring Children: British Immigrant Apprentices to Canada, 1869–1924*. Croom Helm, 1980. Analysis of the life-cycles of 997 Barnardo's children.
- Hodgson, Shirley. *Bristol's pauper children: Victorian education and emigration to Canada*. Bristol Books, 2017. Includes names.

The Australian National Maritime Museum, in conjunction with National Museums Liverpool, provides an interesting online exhibition at:

- On their Own: Britain's Child Migrants
  http://otoweb.cloudapp.net

Hospitals

Voluntary hospitals (in the modern sense) for the sick and infirm were supported by charitable donations. In the nineteenth century, they received more funding than any other charitable cause.[51] All general hospitals were voluntaries, including those with medical schools. So were a variety of hospitals specialising in specific diseases, together with the cottage hospitals which flourished in small towns and rural areas. These hospitals were administered by voluntary lay governors. A few, like London's St Bartholomew's (affectionately known as Barts) were medieval in origin. It was not, however, until the eighteenth century that numbers began to increase. Guy's Hospital in London (1721), the Bristol Royal Infirmary (1735), and the Royal Devon and Exeter Hospital (1743) were among the earliest foundations. By 1800 there were probably about 4,000 beds, with an average occupancy of about 3,000 patients, in voluntary hospitals. Many more were founded in the nineteenth century. The cottage hospital movement took off in the 1860s. By 1891, there were 385 general hospitals, plus many specialist institutions.[52]

Admittance to the voluntary hospitals was generally by ticket from wealthy subscribers. In general, patients were drawn from the 'deserving poor', and not from paupers, who had to make do with whatever care workhouse infirmaries could provide. Originally, hospitals provided care for the sick poor, not for the middle classes and gentry, who were cared for at home. The medical care available in the eighteenth and early nineteenth century was of questionable benefit, and the wealthy were probably better off in their own beds. In 1800, most hospitals admitted patients for 'rest and tendance', rather than for operations or a definite course of treatment.[53] However, advances in care meant that, from the late nineteenth century onwards, hospitals began to attract wealthier patients who were able to pay for their care. That applied not only to the voluntary hospitals, but also to the poor law infirmaries.

Until the early twentieth century, voluntary hospitals led advances in medicine, and provided most medical education. By 1861, 36% of beds were in teaching hospitals, which turned out substantial numbers of trained medics. Many who qualified, but could not find appointments, founded their own hospitals, hoping to make their names in specialist areas such as orthopaedics, maternity care, and ear nose and throat.[54] Others without a place opted to become lowly union medical officers.

The voluntary hospitals did not have a monopoly on care. For the poor needing long-term care in sickness and old age, workhouse infirmaries (see p.96) were the final refuge. Local government also provided lunatic asylums (see p.163–7) and isolation hospitals. The voluntaries were in a minority, and continued to be so until the mid-twentieth century. In 1861, 11,000 patients were in the care of voluntary hospitals, but around 50,000 were cared for by poor law infirmaries.[55] By 1938, the voluntaries had 33% of beds. However, demands for an integrated and rationalised health service, combined with a relative decline in the charity on which they relied, led to sweeping reforms and the creation of the National Health Service by the post-war Labour government.

Details of voluntary hospitals can be traced by searching

- Voluntary Hospitals Database
  www.hospitalsdatabase.lshtm.ac.uk

Their records, including patient records, are listed by

- Hospital Records Database[56]
  www.nationalarchives.gov.uk/hospitalrecords

A number of useful databases are online. Patient records from the Great Ormond Street Hospital, the Evelina and the Alexandra Hip Hospital for Children, and the Royal Hospital for Sick Children, Glasgow are digitised at:

- Historic Hospitals Admission Records Project
  www.hharp.org

The Seamen's Hospital Society was founded in 1821 in order to provide for distressed seamen. It ran a number of hospital ships. Registers of admissions to the Dreadnought Seamen's Hospital are available online at:

- Dreadnought Seamen's Hospital Admissions and Discharges, 1826–1930
  https://search.ancestry.co.uk/search/db.aspx?dbid=61093

Patient records for over 3,000 Woking patients 1885–1908 are indexed by

- Patients in the St Peter's Memorial Home in Woking
  www.surreycc.gov.uk/culture-and-leisure/history-centre/researchers/guides/st-peters-memorial-home

Further Reading
The classic work on hospital history (both voluntary and poor law) is:

- Abel-Smith, Brian. *The Hospitals 1800–1948: a Study in Social Administration in England and Wales.* Heinemann, 1964.

See also:

- Woodward, John. *To do the Sick no Harm: A Study of the British Voluntary Hospital System to 1875.* Routledge & Kegan Paul, 1974.

Social Work
A wide variety of charities engaged in social work of various kinds. Many, as has already been mentioned, visited the poor; many others also created records likely to be of use to family historians. Here it is only possible to mention a small but representative selection.

Church of England Temperance Society
Founded in 1862 to fight the demon drink,[57] this society ran a number of homes for inebriates, and had many local branches. Its volunteer Police Court Missionaries played a major role in founding the probation service. Minutes and papers are held by Lambeth Palace Library **www.lambethpalacelibrary.org**. Local branch records can be identified in the union catalogues listed above, p.3.

Girls Friendly Society
This society was founded in 1875 to offer support and guidance to the large number of working-class girls in the provinces[58] who were moving to urban centres for work. Its central archives are held by the Women's Library at the London School of Economics **www.lse.ac.uk/Library/Collections/Collection-highlights/The-Womens-Library**, but many registers of its members and other records kept by local branches are to be found among parish records and other collections in local record offices.

Houseless Poor Society
The objective of this society, founded in 1820, was to provide refuges for the homeless in London. Its archives, held by London Metropolitan Archives, include admission papers, resident registers, and reports on residents in its various asylums, as well as a range of other administrative papers. The majority relate to the early twentieth century. Full details are given on Aim25 **https://aim25.com**.

Metropolitan Association for Befriending Young Servants
From the 1870s, the importance of assisting ex-workhouse children who had been sent into service by poor law unions was increasingly recognised. The Metropolitan Association for Befriending Young Servants was founded to undertake this role in London; by the 1890s it had over 1,000 volunteers visiting girls in their workplaces. It compiled half-yearly reports on those visited. These reports are frequently found among the records of London Poor Law Unions, some of which have been digitised by Ancestry **www.ancestry.co.uk**. See also:

• Metropolitan Association for Befriending Young Servants (MABYS) **www.childrenshomes.org.uk/MABYS/**

Mothers' Union
The Mothers' Union is a Church of England organisation founded in 1876 in order to bring mothers together in mutual support. By 1914 there were 400,000 members, and most Anglican parishes had a branch.[59] Members signed a card and were 'enrolled'. Minutes, registers and other documents frequently survive among parish and diocesan archives. The central archives are held by Lambeth Palace Library. For a detailed history, see:

- Moyse, Cordelia. *A History of the Mothers' Union: Women, Anglicanism and Globalisation, 1876–2008.* Boydell Press, 2009.

Refuge for the Destitute

The Refuge for the Destitute was opened in London in 1806 in order not only to care for the destitute, but also to reform them. Many of those admitted had just been discharged from the capital's gaols. In the 1810s, judges began to send juvenile offenders to the refuge rather than formally convict them. By the 1820s, most of its inmates were juveniles. Older former prisoners frequently received material assistance, such as the provision of clothing, the purchase of tools, and temporary cash payments. The Male Refuge closed down in 1849, although the Female Refuge continued until 1902.

Those admitted to the Refuge, or supported by it, were expected to provide details of their past as part of the admissions procedure. Their criminal past was fully recorded, but inmates were only admitted if they were thought to be reformable. The decision to accept or reject applicants for admission depended on their 'narratives', which were recorded in the Refuge's minutes. Sometimes additional information on an applicant was sought from other sources; this information was also recorded. The Secretary was not just concerned with admittance procedures. He also needed to record information that might be useful when the time came to place the individual in service or apprenticeship. These mini-biographies, especially earlier ones, contain much valuable information relating to migration, employment, and family history.

The archives of the Refuge, including its minutes, are held by Hackney Archives **www.hackney.gov.uk/archives**. Many 'narratives' taken from the minutes, 1812–27, with other documents, are printed in:

- King, Peter, ed. *Narratives of the Poor in Eighteenth-Century Britain, volume 4: Institutional Responses: the Refuge for the Destitute.* Pickering & Chatto, 2006.

Chapter 4

PAUPERS BEFORE 1834: DOCUMENTING THE OLD POOR LAW

Settlement

The Elizabethan Acts of 1597 and 1601 made the parish the focus of poor law administration. It ordered the appointment of overseers of the poor in every parish; it would be their duty to collect a poor rate and use it to relieve the poor who were settled in their parish. The concept of settlement was central to the operation of the Poor Law, and gained a very precise meaning after the 1662 Act of Settlement and subsequent modifications. Those deemed to be 'settled' in a particular parish included:

- Those born in the parish where their parents had legal settlement, including the illegitimate
- Those who had paid rates in the parish, owned freehold or copyhold property, or rented property for £10 per annum or more
- Serving or former apprentices whose masters had a settlement
- Serving and former parish officers
- Anyone who had been in service in the parish for more than twelve months
- Anyone settled in the parish for more than forty days, provided that they had given notice of their intention to settle

A married woman took her husband's settlement. Children aged seven and under took their parents. Receipt of regular relief from the overseers was seen as recognition of the recipient's right of settlement. If settlement could not be determined, for example, in the case of foundlings, then it was regarded as being wherever the pauper happened to be when he claimed relief.

These rules were remarkably fluid, and were frequently tweaked by both subsequent legislation and case law.[1] They had a significant impact on migration. In particular, overseers were keen to remove any pregnant unmarried woman from their parish, in order to avoid liability for the relief of bastards. Forcible removal of such women was banned in 1732. From 1743, illegitimate children took their settlement from their mothers, not their birth places. There were various other changes. From 1795, only those who had actually claimed relief could be removed. In 1834, a hiring for more than twelve months ceased to give settlement, as did service in a parish office. Settlement law was further refined in 1846 and 1865, by Acts which made those who had lived in a parish for five years (subsequently reduced to one) irremoveable.

The removal of paupers could be expensive. When the Bloodworth family was removed a few hundred yards, from the London parish of St Michael Cornhill to St John the Evangelist, the resultant appeal cost the removing parish £15 4s.[2] The bill for St John the Evangelist was £14 9s 6d. It was in the interests of the overseers to find other ways to achieve the same result. Pressure was put on migrants to move on; they might be given a dole to do so, or relief might simply be refused. Many who were not residing in their parish of settlement were nevertheless given out-relief by that parish, which would have incurred further costs by insisting on residence. Others obtained settlement certificates (see below) from their parish of settlement, guaranteeing that they would not need to claim relief in their parish of residence, and thus obviating the need for removal. Removal was a last resort. It has been estimated that there were, on average, no more than perhaps two removals per year in most parishes.

The 1662 Act gave rise to a number of documents which are important to family and local historians: settlement certificates, settlement examinations, and removal orders. It is important to note that the great majority of these documents relate to migrants rather than to the settled poor.[3] The latter did not need to be examined in order to confirm their settlement, and could not be removed.

Settlement Certificates

After the Act of Settlement 1662, migrants who wished to avoid being troubled by poor law overseers concerning their settlement could obtain a settlement certificate from the churchwardens and overseers of the parish where they were legally settled.[4] The certificate would acknowledge the pauper's eligibility to claim relief in his parish of settlement, and thus absolve the receiving parish of any potential liabilities on that score. After 1697, certificates were frequently written on printed forms. Certificates varied in their content, but normally named the migrant and his family, and identified their parish of settlement; they sometimes also identified the parish to which the family moved (and are most likely to be found among its parish records). Certificates had to be signed by parish officers, plus two Justices of the Peace. From 1697, 'certificate men' who held a valid certificate could not legally be removed from the parish where they were living, unless they claimed relief.

The attitudes of the overseers who were called upon to write certificates varied. If the migrant had promise of employment which might enable him to gain a fresh settlement, then it would be in their interests to provide one. On the other hand, if the migrant was a skilled tradesman whose abilities would be missed if he moved, they might refuse to provide a certificate.

Settlement Examinations

Settlement examinations were normally conducted by two Justices of the Peace. Their aim was to determine the settlement of the pauper being examined. Examinations were conducted not just to effect removal, but also to determine eligibility for relief. The pauper was required to give details of all his movements likely to affect his settlement status. The Justices' clerks recorded the details given. Examinations contain sufficient biographical information to enable the Justice to determine settlement and eligibility for relief – but no more than that. They are therefore somewhat biased mini-biographies, primarily concerned with movements since the last occasion on which a settlement was established, although incidental details may sometimes be recorded. They may record names, ages, places of birth, details of parents, wives, children, and former masters, former places of residence, and details of any apprenticeships served. For example, when William Palmer was examined in Bradford on Avon in 1773, he said that he was aged forty-seven, and had been born in Sturminster Newton. When he was sixteen, he had been 'colted'[5] to John Price, clothier of Wotton-under-Edge, and had served him for just over three of the four years that had been agreed. He had then worked as a journeyman cloth worker, but enlisted in His Majesty's service in around 1755, and was discharged in 1763. Since then he had worked as a journeyman cloth-worker in Bradford.[6]

The settlement of a married woman depended upon her husband's settlement. When Ann Boswell, a widow aged fifty-seven, was examined by a Justice in Chelsea in 1752, she claimed that she had been married twenty-four years earlier to her second husband in the Liberty of the Fleet (and therefore clandestinely[7]). He had held parochial office in Pershore (Worcestershire), and she had lived with him there for thirteen years. She had not since done any act to obtain a fresh settlement, and was 'passed' to Pershore. Incidental information included the fact that her only son was an apprentice.[8]

The determination of settlement could be a difficult task, and could necessitate tracing a family's movements over several generations. George Elson's grandfather acquired a settlement in Lutterworth by apprenticeship. His father never acquired a settlement anywhere else, and when he died George, his mother, and his siblings were removed to Lutterworth. George himself recounted his family's experiences in 1837, and had himself presumably never acquired a settlement anywhere else.[9]

It should be borne in mind that it was open to the examinee to avoid mentioning relevant information, or even to give false information. The Justice was frequently in no position to check the authenticity of the examinee's statements.

Settlement examinations are likely to be found among the parish records of the parish where the examinee was living, although some were sent with removal orders to the parish of settlement. After 1835, they had to be sent with the removal order.[10] Occasionally, they may be found among Quarter Sessions records. It has been estimated that between 150,000 and 200,000 settlement examinations for London survive for the century following 1730.[11] There are many more in the provinces.

Removal Orders

Once a pauper had been examined, and assuming that the place of settlement was elsewhere, the Justice would make a removal order, requiring parish constables to escort the pauper to the parish liable to pay relief. The pauper would be passed from parish constable to parish constable, with the order (which will usually be found among the records of the parish of settlement) until he reached his destination.

Removal orders may be filed separately, but were sometimes attached to settlement examinations, or perhaps written on their backs. They record the names of paupers, their spouses, and their children, if any. They also note the parish from which the pauper was being removed, and the parish to which they were being sent. Sometimes there may be additional details of their circumstances. All the constables who escorted them were expected to sign the removal order, so it is possible to trace the course of the pauper's removal journey. From around 1750, both settlement examinations and removal orders were frequently written on printed forms, at least in Wiltshire.

Removal orders may be found among both parish and Quarter Sessions records. A 1735 order in the Wiltshire sessions papers names Thomas Simons, his wife Anne, a fourteen-year old daughter, Martha, and a five-year old, Anne, who had all 'unlawfully come into the parish of Tisbury'. They were ordered to be removed to Swallowcliffe.[12]

Bastardy

Society took a dim view of bastards. The shame of bastard birth pursued the innocent victim for life. The bastard was the living proof that his parents were sinners; his or her existence threatened the inheritance of legitimate children. The failure to conform to social mores seemed to threaten the natural order of things.

Bastardy was a significant and increasing problem. In the sixteenth century, the rate of bastardy among live births was probably under 2%. By the nineteenth century it had increased to 6.5%.[13] It was the topic of much legislation: Burn's 1780 edition of his handbook on *Justices of the Peace* devoted no fewer than thirty-six pages to the topic. The process of enforcing bastardy legislation was complex and bureaucratic, productive of much paper for researchers to consult.

Overseers were responsible for the maintenance of single mothers and their children. Bastardy could cost them significant amounts of money. Consequently, they made determined efforts to discover the names of fathers, who were required to pay the cost of nursing, and regular maintenance. Justices of the Peace conducted bastardy examinations in order to compel the mother to swear to the name of the father. They also sought to determine the mother's settlement, so that the mother could be removed to the parish which was liable to pay poor relief before the birth. Bastardy examinations can provide much useful information; for example, the 1763 examination of Christian Dew before a Chelsea Justice revealed that she was actually married to Edward Dew, who had left her five years earlier, and was thought to have become a marine on board one of His Majesty's ships. She was now 'pregnant of a bastard child... unlawfully begotten of her body by one Philip Gibson of ...Richmond in the County of Surrey, bricklayer'.

If Justices were unable to discover the name of the father before the birth, the midwife might be instructed to discover the name of the father while the woman was in labour! In 1684, Elizabeth Bushell of Great Bedwyn (Wiltshire) testified that, 'in the greatest of Margaret Blackwell's extremity she did ask her who was the father of the child and her answer was that John Farmer was the only father of the child and this question she put to the said Margaret Blackwell severall times before she was delivered or she would deliver her'.[14] Once parentage was determined, the Justices hearing the case would issue a bastardy order setting out who was to pay for the child's maintenance, and perhaps ordering a whipping for the mother (rarely for the father). The father was compelled to enter a bastardy bond, setting out the amounts he had to pay and the names of his sureties, possibly with further details. If he tried to abscond, he might be faced with a warrant to appear at Quarter Sessions. If he objected to the bond, the overseers could apply for an affiliation order requiring him to sign. If the father could not be found, the child became the responsibility of the parish. An Act of 1609 empowered Justices to send the mothers of chargeable bastards to the House of Correction (see p.31).

Bastardy cases were regularly heard at Quarter Sessions. Its order books and minutes frequently detail the evidence the Bench heard, and the orders it made. The latter, together with bonds and examinations, were frequently kept in parish chests; many can also be found filed with Quarter Sessions rolls and papers (see below, p.125–6).

In the sixteenth century, most cases of bastardy came before the ecclesiastical courts (for their records, see below, p.133–4). That gradually changed in the seventeenth century, as the Elizabethan poor laws took effect, and as overseers realised that Justices of the Peace had the power to take instant effective action, and could impose tougher penalties than ecclesiastical judges. They were available at any time, whereas there were long intervals between the sittings of the church courts. Nevertheless, there was frequently close cooperation between secular and ecclesiastical courts.

Fornication was a sin in the eyes of the church, and until the eighteenth century single mothers were frequently presented by churchwardens at ecclesiastical visitations. Culprits might be punished there and then, or cited to appear before the Archdeaconry or Consistory court at a later date. Penitents might merely be admonished, but were frequently ordered to be humiliated by being dressed in a white sheet, without shoes, and ordered to read a confession in front of the whole parish. In the sixteenth century the fornicator might also receive a beating from the parish priest. For those who could afford to pay, the penance might be commuted to a fine. Relevant records include churchwardens' presentments, citations, act books, and certificates of penances performed. These are to be found among diocesan records.

Bastards, of course, were also entered in parish registers when (and if) they were baptised. It is easy to identify them, as their fathers are rarely named. Mothers are frequently designated with terms such as 'hore' or 'harlot'. Comparison of parish registers with bastardy orders reveals that only a small proportion of illegitimate children became the subject of bastardy orders.[15]

Some parishes kept other records. In London, for example, the overseers of St Clement Danes kept a register of securities, which recorded details of father, mother, the father's securities, and the eventual fate of the child.

For a detailed guide to bastardy records (which includes an appendix giving over seventy synonyms for bastards), see:

- Paley, Ruth. *My Ancestor was a Bastard: a family historian's guide to sources for Illegitimacy in England and Wales*. Rev. ed. Society of Genealogists Enterprises, 2011.

The records of the ecclesiastical courts are described in Chapter 7 of:

- Raymond, Stuart A. *Tracing your Anglican ancestors: a guide for family and local historians*. Pen & Sword, 2017.

Some of the documents that might be produced in a fornication case are illustrated by:

- University of Nottingham. Manuscripts and Special Collections. Penance and Punishment **www.nottingham.ac.uk/manuscriptsandspecialcollections/ exhibitions/online/thebawdycourt/penanceandpunishment.aspx**

Pauper Apprentices

Between the seventeenth and nineteenth century, one of the major problems facing poor law overseers was what to do with pauper children, especially bastards. The law placed responsibility for their maintenance squarely on the overseers, unless they could identify fathers who could be held responsible. Pauper children could be a costly drain on the poor rates. Not only that, the indiscipline of youth was thought to pose a serious threat to society. Youth had to be controlled. Both of these problems were solved by adapting (some would say perverting) the institution of apprenticeship.

Charitable support of poor apprentices has already been discussed. Children able to obtain the sponsorship of a charity were fortunate; they were able to look forward to an apprenticeship which provided them with opportunities equal to those of apprentices whose fathers had paid their own premiums. Pauper apprenticeship frequently (although not always) failed to provide such prospects. Children were bound to the poorest trades, which frequently constituted drudgery. Children as young as seven or eight were bound to husbandry, to housewifery, and to other labour-intensive occupations which required little skill, or which could best be undertaken by children. Children apprenticed to chimney sweeps could learn to climb chimneys for their masters, but it was not a skill they could use as adults. Masters frequently accepted children because they were tempted by the small premium that might be offered, or they needed the abilities which children had, not because they offered a promising career. Overseers were frequently more concerned with getting children off the poor rate than with placing them in a situation which might provide them with future prospects.[16]

The choice of master was up to the overseers. In pauper apprenticeship, prior to 1816, parents had no say. If they refused consent to a binding proposed by the overseers, they lost their entitlement to poor relief. Policy on the placement of apprentices differed from parish to parish. Householders could be compelled to take an apprentice, and in some parishes they were assigned to masters on a rota basis. After 1696, in some places, such fines became an important component of parish income, although attracting much controversy. It was in the interest of the parish to place apprentices with masters who were not parishioners, since any future claim to poor relief would then become the responsibility of the master's parish. During the Industrial Revolution, as textile factories steadily expanded in size, demand for parish apprentices also increased. Pauper children were frequently sent many miles from home to meet this demand, so much so that they lost contact with their families. The practice began in the 1770s, when the overseers of St Clement Danes in London began to apprentice their children to John Birch's cotton mill in Cartmel and, subsequently, Backbarrow (both in Lancashire).[17] The workforce of Toplis & Co. at Cuckney (Nottinghamshire) consisted principally of parish apprentices; some were local, but others came from as far away as London, Essex, Birmingham, Bristol, and Hereford.[18] Between 1784 and 1814, 4,414 children were apprenticed in northern industrial mills.[19]

It was not until the Parish Apprenticeship Act 1816 that Parliament acted to provide greater protection for pauper apprentices. This Act required Justices to consult parents when authorising bindings, and children could not be sent more than forty miles from their home parish.

The master was expected to act *in loco parentis*, and was given total responsibility for his apprentices' lodging, clothing, and food. Apprentices were expected to serve until they reached the age of twenty-four for boys (twenty-one after 1766 in London, and 1778 elsewhere), and twenty-one (or marriage) for girls. How many actually did so is questionable; many absconded, and adverts concerning runaway apprentices frequently appear in nineteenth-century newspapers (see Chapter 10). The conditions in which they served could be appalling: masters and mistresses were frequently more interested in strict obedience and work than in child welfare. In 1767, Mary Clifford's mistress starved and beat her to such an extent that she died. Justice caught up with her: Elizabeth Brownrigg was hanged for murder.[20] It is likely that there were many similar cases where masters or mistresses did not suffer retribution.

The basic document in pauper apprenticeship was the indenture. One copy was kept by the overseers (and can now frequently be found among parish records), while the other was given to the master. Indentures followed a standard format. The information provided was likely to include:

- The name of the pauper (but rarely that of his parents), and his home parish
- The age of the pauper
- Names of overseers, frequently including the names of churchwardens, who were *ex officio* overseers. Justices of the Peace sometimes also signed; after 1816 they were required to sign a separate consent to binding
- The name of the master (and perhaps of his wife)
- The trade which the apprentice was to learn

Occasionally, in the early centuries, pauper apprentices were recorded in borough apprenticeship registers. In a few cases, separate pauper apprenticeship registers were kept; for example, the register at Colyton (Devon) runs from 1598 to 1711.[21] From 1766 in London and Middlesex, and from 1816 elsewhere, overseers were required to keep parish registers of apprentices. These were kept in books of printed forms, and recorded:

- Names of apprentices, their sexes and ages
- Their parents' names and residences
- Names of masters, with their residences and trades
- Term of the apprenticeship
- Any assignment fee paid
- The names of overseers and assenting magistrates

These registers are actually more useful than the indentures themselves, since they record the names of apprentice's parents. From 1844, they were supposed to be kept by Poor Law Guardians, rather than overseers.

Raymond's *My Ancestor was an Apprentice* has already been cited (above, p.48). A briefer introduction to apprenticeship records is provided by:

- How to use Apprentice Records for Genealogy Research
  https://blog.findmypast.com/how-to-find-out-more-about-your-ancestors-using-apprentice-records-2021532877.html

Many parish apprenticeship registers have been published by Devon Family History Society. Ancestry **www.ancestry.co.uk** has databases of Dorset and London poor law records, which include pauper apprenticeship records, 1623–1898. Find My Past **www.findmypast. co.uk** has a variety of poor law databases, some of which include apprenticeship records. The London Lives 1690–1800 website includes pages on 'Researching Apprentices' **www.londonlives.org/static/ Apprentices.jsp**, which includes the apprenticeship register of St Botolph's Aldgate 1777–1805, and various other related sources from London. All of these databases are included in the list at the end of this chapter.

For the history of pauper apprenticeship at the end of the eighteenth century, see:

- Honeyman, Katrina. *Child Workers in England, 1780–1820: Parish Apprentices and the Making of the Early Industrial Labour Force.* Ashgate, 2008.

Overseers and Churchwardens' Accounts

Overseers had considerable financial responsibility. They frequently kept their own accounts, although in smaller parishes these might be merged with the accounts of churchwardens. In his evidence to the Poor Law Commission of 1834, Nassau Senior took a dim view of these accounts: 'no form is prescribed for keeping [them] … sometimes they are merely entered on loose paper … in most cases they consist of a mere day-book of receipt and expenditure without any statement of the grounds on which relief has been afforded, and often without stating even the names of the persons relieved'.[22] The latter omission was in fact illegal; from 1691, the inclusion of a list of those permanently maintained by the parish had been required.[23]

Despite Nassau's comments, accounts do sometimes survive, and the statutory requirement to list parish pensioners was frequently complied with. Overseers' accounts may make it possible to piece together quite detailed pictures of the lives of specific individuals. Overseers were expected to relieve the poor, sometimes with money, sometimes with clothes or housing. They had to pay apprenticeship premiums and other costs associated with the indentures of pauper children. Settlement examinations and removal orders had to be paid for. Accounts frequently record the cost of removing pregnant women from the parish, and thus preventing their bastards becoming a charge on the parish. An alternative was to ensure that the parents of bastards married – which might require the parish to pay for the marriage. This was particularly effective if the father's settlement was elsewhere, as the baby would then take his settlement.

Overseers' accounts record these expenses, and sometimes (but not always) name those who benefited. The 1732 accounts of St Botolph Aldgate, in London, record many 'disbursements to random poor', naming them. In 1733, they relieved 'Mary Mackmannus her Husband being run away'. In 1776, they recorded the expenses of individual paupers sent to the workhouse in Hoxton.[24] The Hindon overseers accounts for 1648 are preserved among Wiltshire Quarter Sessions records.[25] They record, for instance, that Thomas Hewes received 16s 6d relief during the year, and that another 16s was paid for his rent. Others were cheaper: Widow Turner's rent for the whole year was 12s, and Mary Leigh received a mere 3s.

Churchwardens' accounts may also include information regarding paupers, even when there were separate overseers' accounts. In seventeenth-century Devizes (Wiltshire), for example, the churchwardens made numerous payments of small sums to relieve the poor.[26] Many of these were travellers 'with a pass' issued by magistrates, perhaps soldiers, sailors, or men who had been rescued from slavery in North Africa. Unfortunately, none of the 'poore souldiers taken by the Turk' are named. The names of the local poor, however, are frequently given, although not always in full. For example, 'Orchards' was placed as an apprentice with Thomas Phillipps in 1668.[27] Henry Self's child was given 8s 6d 'to carry her to London and for cloaths'. She subsequently received 1s 4d 'for a paire of drawers'.[28] Rebecca Chivers was given 3s, 'being sick'.[29] The rents of poor parishioners were sometimes paid, as were premiums to apprentice pauper children.

Even before the passing of the great Elizabethan poor law Acts of 1597 and 1601, it is possible to identify the poor in churchwardens' accounts. The accounts of Stratton (Cornwall), for example, record the payment of 5s to 'Wylliam Wescot on Candellmas day in his sykness' in 1562.[30] In 1573, Robert Sander was given 18d 'for a pair of schowys for Thomas Clarke'. Shortly after, he was paid the same amount for another pair.[31] The same account records 6d paid to Master Underdon for 'the drawyn of a passe port for Jone Morton'. Four men were subsequently paid to 'bere Jone Morton from Orchard to Borro'.[32] Passes were regularly issued to the poor who had to travel. Overseers and churchwardens frequently provided their bearers with subsistence, and mentioned them in accounts, unfortunately not always naming them.

Constables were also involved in poor law administration. They escorted paupers who were removed, and relieved travellers. Their accounts rarely survive, but when they do they may name those removed, and travellers with passes – although, like the Devizes churchwardens, the Wigginton (Oxfordshire) constables rarely mentioned names.[33]

The accounts of parish waywardens (or highway surveyors) may also identify paupers. They had the responsibility for maintaining parish roads. Overseers frequently required paupers to work under the direction of the waywardens, and this may be reflected in waywardens' accounts.

Vestry Minutes
Parish officers, in theory, were supervised by Justices of the Peace, or, in the case of churchwardens, by bishops and archdeacons. In practice, however, the parish vestry could take a leading role in deciding matters of parish government. Vestry minutes frequently survive from the

---

Some typical extracts from the Wimbledon Vestry minutes:

- 1 March 1746[-7]. 'Wid Lancaster's three children allowed apparel to be clothed according to the rest of the parish children, and to be relieved until the next meeting at the officers' discretion'.
- 4 February 1753. 'Ann Lanchester to be bound out apprentice to Wi Draycutt, Old Street, St Luke's, London, victualler, who keeps the sign of the Cart and Horses'.
- 24 August 1766. 'The churchwardens and overseers are to try the cause of which they have had notice to be tried at Hicks Hall concerning the unjust removal of Catherin Clark from St James's in the liberty of Westminster by order of removal'.
- 19 October 1767. 'Complaint has been made at this meeting by the master of the workhouse in respect of Edw Carter for misbehaviour'.
- 31 July 1768. 'The officers are to take Edward Carter into custody and have him before a JP to desire him to commit him to the house of correction for so long a time as the crime of the complaint will admit'.

From Cowe, F.M., ed. *Wimbledon Vestry Minutes 1736, 1743–1788: a calendar*. Surrey Record Society 25, 1964.

eighteenth and nineteenth century, and may contain a great deal of information about the poor, although of much the same character as that found in accounts.

Lists of Paupers

A number of sixteenth-century towns pioneered the collection of systematic listings of the poor, in order to determine how they should be treated. Options included relief for the old and disabled, apprenticeship for the young, removal for immigrants, or labouring in a bridewell. These census-type listings may give names and ages, details of children, occupations, etc. They survive for a number of boroughs, and some have been published. These include those for Norwich, Ipswich, and Salisbury, listed under further reading below. Similar listings survive for a few rural parishes.[34]

In the late sixteenth century, the vestry of St Saviour, Southwark, ordered its churchwardens to take 'views' of 'newcomers and inmates' every fortnight to identify potential paupers who ought to be removed. A few of these 'views' are transcribed at:

- The Parish of St Saviour, Southwark: Views of Inmates
  www-personal.umich.edu/~ingram/StSaviour/views.html

After 1691, as has already been seen, overseers were legally required to keep lists of paupers for the scrutiny of ratepayers and justices. These were supposed to be reviewed annually by the vestry, and were frequently recorded in account books. Sometimes, these lists are divided into categories, listing separately, for example, 'pensioners', or 'casual poor'. Towards the end of the eighteenth century, these lists were increasingly printed and distributed to ratepayers, who might help the overseers identify the malingerers or fraudulent claimants.[35]

As vestries tried to drive down the cost of poor relief in the late eighteenth and early nineteenth century, they increasingly sought to use these lists to conduct informed reviews of the relief being granted.[36] In London and other urban parishes, alphabetical lists of paupers were frequently written in pre-printed volumes with alphabetic tabs on the edge of the page. Overseers could over time enter details of all their interactions with individual paupers, and in the process compile a ready reference guide to the history of the parish's relationship with them. Similarly, at Broomfield (Somerset), a book labelled 'Allowances of the Poor' was commenced in 1821. This recorded claimants' names, details of their family, and the relief that had been granted. There were columns headed 'character', 'wages', 'employers', 'complaints of the poor', what they were 'allow'd', and 'Why allow'd or disallow'd'. At Wimborne Minster (Dorset), parish officers listed bastard children and those receiving house rents. At Fareham (Hampshire), the parish surgeon was directed to provide lists of all persons 'ill and unable to work on Wednesday morning in every week', prior to the meeting of the select vestry. In 1784, the St Clement Danes (London) overseers took a census of its workhouse population, listing names, ages, and how they gained settlement. This census counted 383 inmates;[37] it is digitised at **www.londonlives.org**.

For a fuller discussion of lists of paupers, with some eighteenth- and early nineteenth-century abstracts from St Clement Danes) and St Botolph Aldgate, see:

- London Lives 1690 to 1800: Lists of Paupers receiving Parish Relief
  www.londonlives.org/static/LP.jsp

Pauper Inventories

Before granting relief, overseers had first to determine whether paupers had any goods, and, if so, what they were worth. Goods could be seized and sold, in order to recompense the parish for expenditure on poor relief. Inventories of paupers' goods might be taken either when relief was claimed, or when the pauper died. Between 1648 and 1766, the goods of forty Frampton (Lincolnshire) paupers were inventoried; they had a combined value of £127.[38] The Frampton overseers were unusual in actually valuing paupers' goods; frequently, no valuation was made in pauper inventories.

Paupers might be permitted to keep their goods until they died, at which point they would be seized and disposed of by the overseers. Sometimes goods were branded with parish marks so that they could not be pawned or sold by the pauper or his family. A few paupers made wills leaving their goods to the overseers. The goods of runaway parents, bastards' fathers, and others, might also be inventoried. They too could have their possessions seized.

Pauper inventories are likely to be found with other poor law papers among parish records, sometimes filed separately, sometimes intermingled with accounts and other papers. Most were made between 1720 and 1770. Inventories provide us with some indication of the material circumstances of our poor ancestors. However, it is not always easy to distinguish pauper inventories from inventories taken for other purposes, such as debt collection.

Pauper Letters

The settlement certificate system (see above) meant that paupers could sometimes expect to receive support from their parish of settlement, despite not living in it. The overseers of 'host' parishes sometimes paid relief and sought reimbursement from the parish of settlement. Alternatively, payment might be made directly. Either way, such out-relief could be beneficial to both overseers and paupers; for the former, it avoided costs which might otherwise be incurred; for the latter it avoided the trauma of removal. It also meant that there was frequent correspondence between paupers and overseers (and also between overseers). Paupers not resident in their parish of settlement frequently lived too far away to apply for relief in person; they had to do so by post. The letters they wrote (or that scribes wrote for them) provide us with a rare direct personal record of what our poorest migrant ancestors felt and thought. They may also identify relatives. Further information might be found in the letters of the overseers, of clergy, and of concerned relatives, friends and neighbours. Many late eighteenth and early nineteenth-century paupers' letters can be found among parish records. These are among the few documents which reveal the actual circumstances of paupers, and the reasons why they claimed relief. They may exaggerate the claims of individual petitioners, and they may on occasion be formulaic or sycophantic, but they do provide a useful indication of the level of poverty thought to merit the granting of relief. In early nineteenth-century Kirkby Lonsdale, for example, paupers' letters suggest that most claims to relief were based on children, incapacity, and unemployment. Weekly pensions, rent, clothing, and medical expenses were the needs most commonly expressed.[39] Accounts, where they survive, may reveal how such needs were met.

Pauper letters seeking relief are frequently found among parish records. So are letters between overseers concerning particular paupers. Record Office catalogues may describe them as paupers' letters, petitions, or vouchers. In Northamptonshire, for example, 2,000 letters have been identified. However, archivists have not always fully catalogued them, and it may be necessary to search through all surviving poor law records to identify letters. Some have been edited in the collections by Levene and Sokoll listed below. Further guidance is provided by:

- King, Steven. 'Pauper Letters as a Source', *Family & Community History* 10(2), 2007, p.167–70.
- Sokoll, Thomas. 'Old Age in Poverty: the Record of Essex Pauper Letters, 1780–1834', in Hitchcock, Tim, King, Peter, & Sharpe, Pamela,

eds. *Chronicling Poverty: the Voices and Strategies of the English Poor, 1640–1840*. Macmillan Press, 1997, p.127–54.
* Sokoll, Thomas. 'Negotiating a Living: Essex Pauper Letters from London, 1800–1834', in Fontaine, Laurence, & Schlumbohm, Jürgen, eds. *Household Strategies for Survival 1600–2000: Fission, Faction and Cooperation*. Cambridge University Press, 2001, p.19–46.
* London Lives 1690–1800: Letters to Parish Officials Seeking Poor Relief **www.londonlives.org/static/PR.jsp**

Workhouse Records
Mention has already been made of the many workhouses built in the eighteenth century and earlier by city Corporations of the Poor, and by both rural and urban parishes. Their records may include admission and discharge registers, lists of inmates, minutes, and a variety of other documents. The admissions register of St Martin in the Fields, for example, records over 10,000 admissions between 1738 and 1748.[40]

The records of Corporations of the Poor are likely to be found among city archives. For Bristol, see Butcher's *Bristol Corporation of the Poor* (below, p.87). Evidence for parish workhouses may sometimes be found among parish records, and especially in overseers' accounts and other poor law records.

A daybook compiled by the master of Knaresborough workhouse, which includes the names of inmates, details of the work they performed, and the resultant income, is held by the Yorkshire Archaeological and Historical Society. It has been published as:

* Garcia-Bermejo Giner, Maria and Montgomery, Michael, eds. *The Knaresborough Workhouse Daybook: Language and Life in 18th Century North Yorkshire*. Quacks Books for the Yorkshire Dialect Society, 2003.

Quarter Sessions Order Books and Rolls
Jurisdiction over the poor law was exercised, in the first instance, by Justices of the Peace and Quarter Sessions.[41] Some matters, for example settlement and bastardy examinations, could be dealt with by one or two Justices, or perhaps at Petty Sessions; others, such as disputes concerning settlement or apprenticeship, went before the full bench at Quarter Sessions. The proceedings of Quarter Sessions were recorded in order books or minutes; the documents produced in court, such as presentments, informations, and petitions, were rolled up together in sessions rolls. Occasionally, individual Justices kept 'justicing books' recording their own decisions.

These documents can provide a great deal of useful information on a wide variety of topics. Disputes about settlement occupied much of the time of Quarter Sessions, and caused the spillage of much ink. Bastardy was another topic which received a great deal of attention. Cases dealing with apprenticeship were also common. A few examples of cases that came before the Justices will demonstrate the amount of information that may be available.

Among the papers of Worcestershire Quarter Sessions is a 1619 order dismissing Edward Brode from the charge of being the father of Bridget Reynold otherwise Tolley's bastard child. The father was found to be John Heath. Nevertheless, Edward Brode was required to maintain the child until he should bring John Heath before the bench.[42]

The Wiltshire order book for 1643 tells us that Elizabeth Davis alias Orpen had borne a bastard child while serving Mr Reade of Purton as a covenant servant. She had been dismissed, and returned to her mother in Wilton. The court ordered that she should be sent back to Purton, where she was to be relieved.[43]

In 1670, the Somerset Quarter Sessions order book records that Mary Periam of Runton had refused to take in John Silvester, a parish apprentice from Upton, who had been assigned to her care by virtue of a tenement she held in Upton. The bench ordered the indenture to be confirmed, and that she should appear before them if she refused.[44]

When settlement was disputed between parishes, Quarter Sessions could order one parish to pay the costs of the other. In 1736, the parish of Orcheston St George (Wiltshire) appealed against an order to remove Elizabeth Robins alias Robertson and her son Alexander from St Edmunds, Salisbury. But they had to maintain the pauper until their appeal was heard. When it was successful, the overseers of St Edmunds were ordered to reimburse their Orcheston counterparts for the poor relief they had paid, amounting to twenty shillings.[45]

It was also possible for Quarter Sessions to order a man and his wife to be split up. When in 1736 the Winsome (Wiltshire) overseers appealed against an order to remove John Speake and his wife Martha from Hindon, the court decided that John should be removed, but Martha should not.[46]

William White, JP, was one of those who kept his own 'justicing book'. In 1745 he recorded that he had summonsed the overseers of Tilshead (Wiltshire) to 'show cause' why they had refused poor relief to Frances Whitley and Mary Found, paupers of their parish. They agreed to do so.[47]

Unfortunately, documents such as these are frequently not very well indexed, except when they have been published or digitised. Nevertheless, the information they contain may be invaluable.

Further Reading

The poor law has been studied from a variety of perspectives. The classic work by the Webbs is an administrative study. But it is also possible to view the poor law as a legal system, or to study it from the perspective of the poor. Different authors take different approaches.[48] Perhaps the best, if rather dated, introduction written specifically for the local historian, and covering the whole period of the old poor law, is:

- Oxley, Geoffrey W. *Poor relief in England and Wales 1601–1834*. David & Charles, 1974.

The prelude to the Elizabethan poor law is discussed in:

- McIntosh, Marjorie Keniston. *Poor Relief in England 1350–1600*. Cambridge University Press, 2012.

The early centuries of the old poor law are dealt with in:

- Slack, Paul. *The English Poor Law 1531–1782*. Cambridge University Press, 1995.
- Hindle, Steve. *On the parish? The micro-politics of poor relief in rural England c.1550–1750*. Clarendon Press, 2004.

For the poor law in the eighteenth-century, and for its nineteenth-century replacement, see:

- Brundage, Anthony. *The English Poor Laws, 1700–1930*. Palgrave, 2002.
- Lees, Lynn Hollen. *The Solidarities of Strangers: The English Poor Laws and the People, 1700–1948*. Cambridge University Press, 1998.
- King, Steven. *Poverty and Welfare in England 1700–1850: a Regional Perspective*. Manchester University Press, 2000.

For an older classic, see:

- Webb, Sidney, & Webb, Beatrice. *English Poor Law History*. 2 pts. in 3 vols. Reprinted Frank Cass & Co., 1963. Pt.1. The Old Poor Law. Pt.II. The Last Hundred Years.

The state of the poor, and of poor law administration, at the end of the old poor law is tendentiously but influentially described in the report of the Royal Commission, now available in a modern edition:

- Checkland, S.G., & E.O.A., eds. *The Poor Law Report of 1834*. 2nd ed. Penguin, 1974. Many volumes of the original report are digitised at **https://archive.org**. Appendix B includes the replies of over 1,600 parishes to questions posed by the Commission.

On the law of settlement, see:

- Taylor, J.S. *Poverty, migration and settlement in the industrial revolution: sojourners' narratives*. Society for the Promotion of Science and Scholarship, 1989.

For basic introductions to poor law records, see also the works by Fowler and Simon mentioned above, p.37. There is also much detailed information in Burlison's work (see p.37 also).
Many facsimiles of poor law documents are printed in:

- Hawkings, David T. *Pauper Ancestors: A Guide to the Records Created by the Poor Laws in England and Wales*. History Press, 2011.

Guides to settlement papers and overseers' accounts are included in:

- Thompson, K.M. *Short guides to records. Second series guides 25–48*. Historical Association, 1997.

Published Sources
Many pauper letters are printed in:

- King, Steven, Nutt, Thomas, & Tomkins, Alannah, eds. *Narratives of the Poor in Eighteenth-Century Britain. Vol. 1: Voices of the Poor: Poor Law Depositions and Letters*. Pickering & Chatto, 2006.

Many local poor law records have been published or digitised. These are listed here:

Bedfordshire
- *Emmison, F.G. 'The Relief of the Poor at Eaton Socon, 1706–1834'*, Publications of the Bedfordshire Historical Record Society 15, 1933, p.1–98. Abstracts rather than transcripts.

Devon
- *Ashton apprentices register, 1804–1841*. Devon Family History Society, 2005. There are similar volumes covering Ashwater, 1803–1831,

Awliscombe, 1803–1839, Bere Ferrers, 1805–1817, Bradninch, 1822–1844, Branscombe, 1808–1833, Broadhempston, 1802–1842, Buckfastleigh, 1833–1844, Burlescombe, 1803–1835, Clyst St Mary, 1804–1831, Cockington, 1803–1842, Coffinswell, 1804–1826, Dalwood, 1804–1827, Dawlish, 1833–1834, Dunchideock, 1807–1832, East Budleigh, 1802-1937, Gidleigh, 1803–1841, Gittisham 1803–1838, Harpford, 1804–1839, Holne, 1804–1830, Huntsham 1744–1811, Ide, 1805–1835, Kenton, 1801–1810, 1811–1820, 1821–1830, & 1831–1840, Kingsteignton 1775–1823, Littleham & Exmouth 1800–1834, Luffincott, 1808–1827, Lustleigh, 1803–1833, Lympstone, 1802–1837, Meeth 1803–1840, Modbury, 1833–1839, Payhembury, 1802–1834, Rose Ash, 1803–1844, Seaton & Beer, 1803–1829, Shillingford St George, 1807–1832, Stockland, 1803–1830, Tormoham, 1803–1836, Whitestone 1803–1839, and Withycombe Raleigh, 1800–1834.

Dorset
- Dorset, England, Poor Law and Church of England Parish Records, 1511–1997
  https://search.ancestry.co.uk/search/db.aspx?dbid=2164
- Dorset, England, Poor Law Settlement and Removal Records, 1682–1862
  https://search.ancestry.co.uk/search/db.aspx?dbid=60673
- Dorset, England, Poor Law Apprenticeship Records, 1623–1898
  https://search.ancestry.co.uk/search/db.aspx?dbid=61226

Essex
- Sokoll, Thomas, ed. *Essex Pauper Letters, 1731–1837*. Records of Social and Economic History, new series 30. Oxford University Press, 2001.

Gloucestershire and Bristol
- Butcher, E. E., ed. *Bristol Corporation of the Poor: selected records 1696–1834*. Bristol Record Society 3. 1932.
- Gray, Irvine, ed. *Cheltenham settlement examinations, 1815–1826*. Bristol & Gloucestershire Archaeological Society Records Section 7. 1969.
- Wilkins, H.J., ed. *Transcription of the Poor Book of Westbury on Trym, Stoke Bishop, and Shirehampton, from A.D. 1656–1698*. Bristol: J.W. Arrowsmith, 1910.

Hampshire
- *Willis, Arthur J., ed.* Winchester settlement papers 1667–1842, from records of several Winchester parishes. The Author, 1967.

Hertfordshire
- Falvey, Heather, & Hindle, Steve, eds. *This Little Commonwealth: Layston Parish Memorandum Book 1607–c.1650 & 1704–c.1747*. Hertfordshire Record Publications 17. 2003.

Lancashire
- Hindle, G.B. *Provision for the relief of the poor in Manchester 1754–1826*. Chetham Society 3rd series 23. 1976. Includes a useful bibliography.

Lincolnshire
- Lincolnshire Settlement Certificates 1675–1860
  https://search.findmypast.co.uk/search-world-records/lincolnshire-settlement-certificates-1675-1860

  Find My Past also has 'Lincolnshire Settlement Examinations 1721–1861', and 'Lincolnshire Poor Law Removals 1665–1865'.

London
- London Lives 1690 to 1800: Crime, Poverty and Social Policy in the Metropolis
  www.londonlives.org/index.jsp

  Includes many digitised records of paupers, including settlement certificates and examinations, removal orders, workhouse admission registers, etc., for a few parishes.

- London, England, Selected Poor Law Removal and Settlement Records, 1698–1930
  https://search.ancestry.co.uk/search/db.aspx?dbid=2651

  Note that this includes examinations and removal orders made under the new poor law.

Middlesex
- Hitchcock, Tim, & Black, John, eds. *Chelsea settlement and bastardy examinations, 1733–1766*. London Record Society 33. 1999.
- Chelsea .Workhouse Admissions and Discharges, 1743–1799
  http://workhouses.org.uk/Chelsea/Chelsea1743.shtml

  For settlement and bastardy examinations, 1733–1750, see **/Chelseabas. shtml**

Norfolk

- Pound, J.F., ed. *The Norwich census of the poor 1570.* Norfolk Record Society, 40. 1971. The data in this book (but not the introduction) is digitised at **http://welbank.net/norwich/1570**

Somerset

- High Littleton & Hallatrow History and Parish Records: The Poor Law, Overseers and the Vestry
  www.highlittletonhistory.org.uk/poorlaw.html

  Numerous transcripts of poor law records, including settlement examinations, removal orders, vestry minutes, etc. Also useful for the post-1834 period.

Suffolk

- Webb, John, ed. *Poor relief in Elizabethan Ipswich.* Suffolk Records Society 9. 1966. The data in this book (but not the introduction) is digitised at **https://search.ancestry.co.uk/search/db.aspx?dbid=7465**

Sussex

- Pilbeam, Norma, & Nelson, Ian, eds. *Poor Law records of Mid-Sussex 1601–1835.* Sussex Record Society 83. 1999.
- Database of Poor Law Records for West Sussex
  www.sussexrecordsociety.org/dbs/pl
  Over 14,000 records, including settlement examinations, removal orders, bastardy orders, and pauper indentures.
- Pratt, Malcolm, ed. *Winchelsea Poor Law Records 1790–1841.* Sussex Record Society 94, 2012.

Warwickshire

- Warwickshire, England, Parish Poor Law, 1546–1904
  https://search.ancestry.co.uk/search/db.aspx?dbid=2421

Wiltshire

- Slack, Paul, ed. *Poverty in early Stuart Salisbury.* Wiltshire Record Society 31. 1975.
- Hembry, Phyllis, ed. *Calendar of Bradford on Avon settlement examinations and removal orders 1725–98.* Wiltshire Record Society, 46. 1990.
- Church, Rosemary, ed. *A Miscellany of Bastardy Records for Wiltshire Volume 1. 1728 to 1893.* Wiltshire Family History Society, 1997. There are a further eight volumes in this series of indexes.

Yorkshire

- West Yorkshire, England, Select Poor Law and Township Records, 1663–1914
  https://search.ancestry.co.uk/search/db.aspx?dbid=9017
  Despite the title, the records in this database probably begin in around 1770.

- West Yorkshire, England, Bastardy Records, 1690–1914
  https://search.ancestry.co.uk/search/db.aspx?dbid=2582

Chapter 5

PAUPERS AFTER 1834: DOCUMENTING THE NEW POOR LAW

Boards of Guardians and the Poor Law Commissioners created a wide range of records, many of which include the names of paupers. They also compiled a variety of records relating to staff, accommodation, finance, and other matters. Unfortunately, many of these records have been lost. Many, however, survive, and are now available for research. It is worth looking out for those discussed below. For records of pauper lunatics, see Chapter 10. Some documents produced under the old poor law continued to be used, and changed little; for example, settlement certificates, settlement examinations, and removal orders. For these, see the previous chapter.

Poor Law Union records are generally held in local record offices; the records of the Commission and its successor bodies are in the National Archives. An extensive listing of surviving records is included in:

- Gibson, Jeremy, et al. *Poor Law Union records.* 2nd/3rd eds. 4 vols. Federation of Family History Societies/Family History Partnership, 1997–2014.

Brief details of surviving records are also given on the local pages of

- The Workhouse
  www.workhouses.org.uk

A full listing of Poor Law Unions, showing the parishes in each union, can also be consulted at:

- List of Poor Law Unions in England
  https://en.wikipedia.org/wiki/List_of_poor_law_unions_in_England

Specific categories of documents created by unions and others are discussed below. However, a few online hosts offer a wide range of digitised documents from specific unions. See, for example:

- Medway, Kent, England, Poor Law Union Records, 1836–1937
  https://search.ancestry.co.uk/search/db.aspx?dbid=60655
- Swansea and Surrounding Area, Wales, Poor Law Union Records, 1836–1916
  https://search.ancestry.co.uk/search/db.aspx?dbid=61232

Birth and/or baptism registers

Workhouse masters were expected to keep registers of births and/or baptisms of workhouse inmates. In the early years, some events recorded in these registers were not entered in the civil registers. Birth registers are likely to record the baby's name, the name(s) of parents, the date of birth, whether the child was legitimate, and the parish to which the parents belonged. Sometimes the date and place of baptism was also recorded. Workhouse registers frequently also record 'discharged with the mother before baptised'.[1] Usually, baptism took place in the local parish church, which means that its register should also be checked for workhouse children's baptisms. The baptismal register of St Matthew's, Exeter, a short walk away from Exeter Workhouse, is full of baptismal entries for workhouse babies, and indeed its gallery was probably built to accommodate workhouse children.

Occasionally, baptism took place privately in the workhouse (usually because the baby was ill). A few workhouses, however, had their own chapels, where baptism could take place if the bishop provided a licence.

Some workhouse registers have been digitised. See, for example:

- Cheshire Workhouse Registers: Baptisms
  www.findmypast.co.uk/articles/world-records/full-list-of-united-kingdom-records/institutions-and-organisations/cheshire-workhouse-records-baptisms
  Covers 1880–1910. Find My Past also has birth and baptism registers from Guildford Union, 1866–1910.

Death Registers

The records of Boards of Guardians frequently include registers of deaths which took place in the workhouse. Workhouse registers give names, ages, death dates, and parishes. These are not, however, normally registers of burials. Burials would normally have taken place in parish churchyards or municipal cemeteries, and be recorded in their registers. However, a few workhouses had their own burial grounds.

Deaths were sometimes also recorded in the minutes of Boards of Guardians (see below). Those that involved a coroner's inquest were reported to the central authorities, and may be recorded in their correspondence files (see below, p.102–4).[2] Find My Past has digitised workhouse burial registers from Cheshire, and minute books from the Farnham Union, in addition to the baptism registers mentioned above.

Admission, Discharge, Creed and other Registers

The information provided by workhouse admission and discharge registers changes over time, but they are likely to list the names of paupers, their dates of admission, ages, occupations, religion, and the parish liable to support them. There may also be notes on the pauper's character and other observations. On 13 April 1836, for example, Louisa Appleby, a 28-year-old widow settled at Beenham, was admitted to the Bradfield Union Workhouse. The admission book records 'her temper so bad her father will not have her at home'. The same volumes recorded discharges, usually giving dates, parishes, and the reason for discharge. Appleby was discharged on 23 January 1837, 'gone to reside with her mother at Midgham and work in the paper mill'. She was again described as 'clean but very indolent and of bad temper'.[3]

Application and report books, and relieving officers' reports, may give more detailed information. These were intended to provide relieving officers with all the information they needed to determine their decisions, and recorded details of applicants' households, disabilities, health, wages, length of residence in the union, resources, and claims for aid.[4] There may also be separate registers for children admitted to workhouse schools, and for tramps (frequently referred to as casuals, or wayfarers). The latter might distinguish ex-servicemen. Sometimes, there may also be registers of paupers' next-of-kin.

A number of admission and discharge registers have been digitised. See:

- Cheshire Workhouse Records (Admissions and Discharges)
  www.findmypast.co.uk/articles/world-records/full-list-of-united-kingdom-records/institutions-and-organisations/cheshire-workhouse-records-admissions-and-discharges

Find My Past also hosts admission and discharge registers from Bury, Chertsey, Manchester, Portsmouth, and Westminster.

- London, England, Workhouse Admission and Discharge Records, 1764–1930
  https://search.ancestry.co.uk/search/db.aspx?dbid=60391
  This includes some registers for workhouses established under the old poor law.

Application and report books for Dorking Union are also available at Find My Past:

- Dorking Poor Law Union Application and Report Books 1837–1947
  www.findmypast.co.uk/articles/world-records/full-list-of-united-kingdom-records/institutions-and-organisations/dorking-poor-law-union-application-and-report-books-1837-1847

Similar databases for Godstone Poor Law Union, 1869–1915, and for Richmond Poor Law Union 1870–1911, are also on Find My Past. A number of relevant indexes are available at:

- Surrey Records Online
  www.surreycc.gov.uk/culture-and-leisure/history-centre/researchers/guides/poor-law-records/dorking

The Derby Union's relieving officers' reports for 1842, relating to 2,235 claimants, have been digitised at:

- Derbyshire Workhouse Reports
  www.findmypast.co.uk/articles/world-records/full-list-of-united-kingdom-records/institutions-and-organisations/derbyshire-workhouse-reports

From 1869, the workhouse master had to record the religious adherence of each new inmate in a creed register, so that appropriate arrangements could be made in case of sickness or death. The register was also used to determine educational provision for children, and was usually open to inspection by ministers of all denominations seeking to identify new arrivals of their persuasion. It recorded the date of the entry, the date of admission, the name of the pauper, 'from whence admitted', their religious creed, the name of the informant, and the date of discharge or death. If the latter is blank, that is likely to indicate that the inmate was still in the workhouse when the next creed register was started. Occasionally, creed registers may also record a pauper's occupation, their last address, and the name and address of their nearest relative. Sometimes they are easier to use than admission and discharge books, as they have a semi-alphabetical arrangement. Some 17,000 entries are recorded in:

- Bury Workhouse Creed Register
  www.findmypast.co.uk/articles/world-records/full-list-of-united-kingdom-records/institutions-and-organisations/bury-workhouse-creed-registers
  This website also hosts a database of around 13,000 names from Cheshire creed registers.

There may be other registers of indoor paupers. For example, registers of the employment of children, and of children boarded out or fostered, were sometimes kept.

Indoor and Outdoor Relief Lists

A printed list of inmates was compiled from admission and discharge registers every six months. Some were indexed, and can be used as a rough index to admission and discharge registers. They should record the names of paupers, whether they were able-bodied, adults or children, their occupations, dates of birth, and religion, although not all of this information was always given. For example, the Chippenham (Wiltshire) Union list of indoor poor for the six months to Michaelmas 1869 records that Eliza Ludlow of Box was maintained in the workhouse for two days in that period, whereas John Tinson was an inmate for 189 days – the whole period.[5] A similar document was provided by the list of 'children in homes schools and institutions' for Chippenham Union at Michaelmas 1891. It named nine children, identifying the institutions in which they had been placed.[6]

Applicants for outdoor relief normally had to appear before the Guardians in person. Out-relief books record names of paupers, ages, parishes of residence, the causes of seeking relief, and what relief was given.

Personal details may sometimes also be provided by applications for relief. London Metropolitan Archives, for example, hold many applications from Poplar, c.1893–1912.

Notices of Chargeability and Removal

The 1834 Act required churchwardens to send a Notice of Chargeability (often on a printed form) before removing paupers to their parish of settlement. Copies of settlement examinations and removal orders (see above, p.70–72) are likely to be attached. Such notices are likely to be found among parish records. They should name the pauper, the parish of settlement, and the overseers of the removing parish. Some examples are transcribed at **www.highlittletonhistory.org.uk/poorlaw.html** (click 'Removals to HL 1676–1863').

From 1865, pauper removals became the responsibility of Guardians, and therefore the notices identify them, and are found among union records.

Medical Records

Improvements in medical care were one of the most important, if unexpected, results of the legislation of 1834. The Poor Law Commissioners had given no thought to the needs of the sick poor. Nevertheless, as has already been seen, workhouses had beds for around 50,000 patients by 1861. Many suffered ailments which the voluntary hospitals were unable to deal with, for example, infectious diseases. Virtually all unions built infirmaries in which the sick poor could be cared for. They also kept records of patients. Registers of the sick might be maintained separately. A General Medical Order issued in 1842 required medical officers to make a weekly return of paupers visited. Medical examination books and medical relief books were also kept. Medical officers might compile reports on diseases. All of these records are likely to be among union records in local record offices.

Many poor law infirmaries became National Health Service hospitals. For example, Plymouth General Hospital at Freedom Fields was founded as the Plymouth Poor Law Institution in 1859. Some retained their own records, although many have since deposited them in local record offices. These records may include admission and discharge registers and other patient records. Many are listed by

• Hospital Records Database
  www.nationalarchives.gov.uk/hospitalrecords/

Bastardy Records

For a few years after 1834, the fathers of bastards were effectively absolved of any responsibility for their maintenance. Mothers became solely responsible, and could not themselves seek any maintenance. If they were destitute they had to enter the workhouse. If they did so, Guardians could seek affiliation orders against fathers at Quarter Sessions, but the need for evidence of paternity to be 'corroborated in some material particular' meant that orders were difficult to obtain. An Act of 1839 removed jurisdiction to Petty Sessions, but it was not until the Bastardy Act 1845 that fathers were again held responsible. This Act took proceedings out of the hands of Guardians and Overseers, and enabled mothers to seek affiliation orders at Petty Sessions.

Applications, registers of summonses issued, and adjudications, may still survive. They are likely to be written on pre-printed forms that have frequently been filed by date, perhaps bound. Applications were frequently filed in two series: those made before births, and those made after. Between 1844 and 1858, returns of orders made had to be sent annually to the Clerk of the Peace. These bastardy returns name mothers and fathers, state the amount of maintenance to be paid, give dates of summonses and hearings, and record the adjudication. They may be useful where Petty Sessions records are not available.

Appeals against orders were heard by Quarter Sessions; annual lists of these were also made. Where mothers were forced to enter the workhouse, Guardians' minutes and other union records may provide information. Consultation of these documents is likely to provide much useful information, for example, the names and addresses of both mothers and fathers, fathers' occupations, dates of summonses and adjudications, dates of birth, and much other useful information. Occasionally, Petty Session minute books recording full details of evidence heard may be found.

Unfortunately, it is unlikely that any of these records will be indexed by name. Those records which survive are found among Quarter Sessions records in local record offices. Bear in mind, too, that Petty Sessions hearings may be reported in newspapers. Many can now be searched online; see, for example, the British Newspaper Archive **www. britishnewspaperarchive.co.uk**.

For Warwickshire, nineteenth-century bastardy records are indexed at:

• Warwickshire Bastardy Indexes 1844–1914
  www.findmypast.co.uk/articles/world-records/full-list-of-united-kingdom-records/institutions-and-organisations/warwickshire-bastardy-index

Pauper Apprenticeship Records
Under the new poor law, the system of pauper apprenticeship described in the previous chapter continued, albeit with some reluctance from the Poor Law Commission and its successors. The responsibility for apprenticing paupers was transferred from the overseers to the unions

in 1844. From that date, pauper apprenticeship indentures, and registers of pauper apprentices may be found among union records. From 1844, the Poor Law Commissioners ordered that no child under nine was to be apprenticed, and that children had to be sufficiently literate to be able to read their own indentures before they entered apprenticeship. Compulsory apprenticeship was abolished for those over fourteen. The Poor Law (Apprentices) Act 1851 made mistreatment of paupers an offence, and required union relieving officers to visit them regularly. Registers of visits to apprentices, and to young servants placed by unions, were sometimes kept. Registers of children placed in service had to be kept from 1851.

In the later nineteenth century, unions were placed under increasing pressure to train workhouse children in their own industrial schools,[7] rather than apprenticing them. Nevertheless, pauper apprenticeship did not finally end until the twentieth century. The York Guardians' register of apprentices carries on right up until 1929, the year in which unions were abolished.[8] The operation of the system in its last few decades is described by:

- Horn, Pamela. 'Youth Migration: the fisher boy apprentices of Grimsby, 1870–1914', *Genealogists' magazine*, 25(3), 1995, p.99–105.

School Records

Unions were required to provide at least three hours of schooling every day for children in their care. Children were to be taught 'reading, writing, arithmetic, and the principles of the Christian Religion, and such other instruction as may fit them for service, and train them to habits of usefulness, industry and virtue'.[9] Registers of children admitted to workhouse schools were kept. For the registers of London's School Districts, see

- London, England, Poor Law School District Registers, 1852–1918
  https://search.ancestry.co.uk/search/db.aspx?dbid=61452

There were also registers of children sent to other institutions, such as industrial schools and (after 1862) certified schools. Industrial schools are listed by Missing Ancestors **www.missing-ancestors.com**. Chippenham Union's archives include a 'list of paupers maintained in institutions and certified schools during the year ended 31st March 1912'.[10] The admissions register of Mayford Industrial School, which catered for the pauper boys of Surrey from 1885, is digitised at **www.findmypast.co.uk/articles/**

Children at Crumpsall Workhouse, c.1895.

world-records/full-list-of-united-kingdom-records/institutions-and-organisations/mayford-industrial-school-admissions-1895-1907.
Many boys were sent to learn seamanship on training ships. A list of these is given at **www.childrenshomes.org.uk/TS**. The records of the Metropolitan Asylums Board, for example, includes registers of boys on the Training Ship *Exmouth*, 1876–1947, as well as a variety of other *Exmouth* records.[11]

In the later nineteenth century, Guardians increasingly sent their children to local National (Anglican) or British (Nonconformist) schools (see above, p.49). After 1873, increasing numbers were sent to the new Board Schools. In 1890, some 200 workhouse schools were in operation. By 1900 numbers had reduced to forty-five.[12]

School registers and log books, both of which record much information about pupils, are held by local record offices. See, for example:

- Horn, Pamela, ed. *Village Education in Nineteenth Century Oxfordshire: the Whitchurch School Log Book.* Oxfordshire Record Society, 51. 1979.
- London, England, School Admissions and Discharges, 1912–1918 **https://search.ancestry.co.uk/search/db.aspx?dbid=61572**
- Somerset, England, School Registers, 1860–1914 **https://search.ancestry.co.uk/search/db.aspx?dbid=61024**

Board of Guardians Minutes

The Minutes of Boards record the business they transacted. They are perhaps the commonest type of workhouse record to survive, and are particularly valuable when they can be read in conjunction with the correspondence in the National Archives, class MH 12. Minutes are frequently voluminous, but follow a standard pattern, and are sometimes indexed. They may mention the names of paupers admitted and discharged, or pauper children apprenticed. They may record interesting anecdotal information about troublesome paupers, including any punishments meted out. Occasionally lists of paupers may be found.

The minutes of sub-committees may also be useful. Large unions were likely to have a House Committee for Workhouse management, a series of relief committees to interview applicants for relief, a boarding-out committee for supervising fostered children, a finance committee, and a range of other committees.[13] The Visiting Committee, consisting of several guardians, was supposed to visit the workhouse weekly; the results of its inspection were supposed to be recorded in a separate Visitors' Book. The minutes of sub-committees may provide much personal information.

Minutes may frequently be supplemented by reports of Guardians' meetings in newspapers (see below, p.169–70). These are likely to give much more detail of the discussions which preceded decisions, but Boards were slow to allow reporters admittance to their meetings, so such reports may not commence until the 1890s or even later. Minutes are discussed in detail by:

- Coleman, Jane M. 'Guardians minute books', in Munby, Lionel M., ed. *Short guides to records*. Historical Association, 1972, separately paginated.

Find My Past has digitised:

- Hambledon Board of Guardians Minute Books 1836–1910
  www.findmypast.co.uk/articles/world-records/full-list-of-united-kingdom-records/institutions-and-organisations/hambledon-board-of-guardians-minute-books-1836-1910
  Minute books from Farnham Union 1872–1910 are also available on this website.

Punishment Books

These recorded the names of workhouse inmate offenders, and identified their offences and punishments. Punishments were inflicted in accordance with a code developed by the Poor Law Commissioners. In their seventh report, the Commissioners noted that 'in consequence of some recent instances of excessive improper punishments inflicted by masters of Workhouses upon some of the pauper inmates', their code had to be revised. Punishment was inflicted for a variety of reasons: fighting, swearing, assault, damaging union property, absconding, etc. The punishment book of the Axbridge Union in 1869, for example, records John Addicott repeatedly 'refusing positively to do work', and being locked up for the day. In 1870, Jane Tilley, presumably a child, was locked up and 'caned by schoolmaster' for her 'Insolence to the Master'. The schoolmaster also caned a number of boys 'for stealing apples from Mr. Day's orchard'.[14] Sometimes paupers' diets were restricted for a time; in more serious cases they might be placed in solitary confinement for a few hours. The most serious cases were taken before magistrates, and thus are likely to be recorded among Quarter Sessions records. A transcript of a punishment book can be consulted at:

• Llandilofawr Union Workhouse
  www.llandeilo.org/workhouse1.html

Vaccination Registers

State sponsored vaccination of children against smallpox began in 1840, and became compulsory for all children – not just paupers – in 1853.[15] It continued until 1948. Children had to be no more than six weeks old. Vaccination officers were appointed by Poor Law Guardians, and consequently vaccination registers are found among union records, although it was not necessary to be a pauper to be vaccinated. Registers record the names of children vaccinated, giving their place and date of birth, their father's name and occupation, or, if the child was illegitimate, the mother's name. The date of vaccination, and the name of the vaccinator, was also recorded. Details of children who died prior to vaccination are also given. These registers virtually duplicate the civil registers of births. A number of vaccination registers have been digitised:

• Newport Pagnell, Buckinghamshire, England, Vaccination Register, 1909–1927
  https://search.ancestry.co.uk/search/db.aspx?dbid=34818

- Surrey Poor Law Union vaccination registers 1872 to 1909
  **www.surreycc.gov.uk/culture-and-leisure/history-centre/researchers/
  guides/poor-law-records/surrey-poor-law-union-vaccination-
  registers-1872-to-1910**

Other Union Records

Unions kept a wide variety of other records. For example, a list of children
bound out by Chippenham Union at 31 March 1912 gives thirty-seven
names, and includes the names of foster mothers with their addresses.[16]
Similarly, documents from Alderbury Union (Wiltshire)[17] include late
nineteenth-century lists of non-resident poor, 'persons in respect of
whom extra medical fees were paid', 'lunatic paupers in the Asylums
chargeable to the Union', 'cases attended by midwives', and boarded-
out children. The minutes of its boarding-out committee include many
reports on individual children, for example:

> 13 Apil 1904. Joseph Underwood. The Clerk produced a letter from
> Mr J.E.Gordon stating that this boy has now recovered from the
> affection of the eyes, but is rather backward in intelligence for his age.

Other records which may be encountered include porter's books
recording the names of visitors, complaint books (although these are
likely to be relatively empty – paupers' complaints were unlikely to be
heard), and a variety of different accounts. Letters from paupers, similar
to those received by overseers prior to 1834, were sometimes received,
although some were also addressed to the poor law authorities in London
(see below). Many unions maintained union letter books, which might
include letters from both the Poor Law Commission (and its successors),
and paupers, as well as other correspondence. It would perhaps be
impossible to compile a full listing of the types of records which might
be available, but Gibson has made a much more valiant attempt than can
be made here.[18]

Poor Law Commission Correspondence and other Papers

Over 16,000 volumes of correspondence between the Poor Law
Commission (and its successors) and Boards of Guardians, covering the
period 1834–1900, are preserved in the National Archives, class MH 12.
These volumes include not only letters received, but also copies of replies
sent. Replies may also sometimes be found among union records in local
record offices. Post-1900 correspondence has mostly been destroyed,
although a small quantity can be found in MH 68.

MH 12 volumes include letters from parish overseers and vestries, poor law inspectors, paupers,[19] and others. In 1836 and 1837, for example, many Norfolk poor petitioned for assistance to emigrate.[20] Sometimes much detail concerning individual paupers is given. Eliza Wood of Cruwys Morchard (Devon), for example, wrote describing herself as 'the unfortunate mother of three idiots'. Efforts had been made to remove her, despite the fact that she kept the parish school.[21]

MH 12 also includes a variety of returns and reports, sometimes listing names. Returns of pauper lunatics (see below, p.163–7), and of children vaccinated (see above), were made regularly. 'Workhouse Inspection Reports' were submitted by Poor Law inspectors after their regular six-monthly visit to each workhouse. Auditors reported on financial matters. Details of workhouse staff can be found on staff appointment forms, and in other papers. Lists of paupers assisted to emigrate were sometimes compiled (see Chapter 10). In 1889, for example, a report on children sent to Canada included the information that Edward Bellow, aged eleven, from Kensington, had been placed with Joseph Langdon of Ameliasburgh Township; he was described as 'self willed but improving. Healthy lad, in good home, generally gives satisfaction, will attend school during winter, pleased with place'.[22] In 1846, some unions made returns of the wives and children of convicts who had been transported.

These records are frequently tightly bound and may be difficult to use. However, a few records from MH 12 have been digitised, and can be downloaded. These are listed at **www.nationalarchives.gov. uk/help-with-your-research/research-guides/poverty-poor-laws**. A subject index appears in MH 15. Papers are organised by union, so it is necessary to determine which union a particular place belonged to. Some correspondence may also occasionally be found in local record offices.

A detailed discussion of the MH 12 correspondence is provided by:

- Carter, Paul & Whistance, Natalie. *Living the Poor Life: a guide to the Poor Law Union Correspondence c.1834–1871 held at the National Archives.* British Association for Local History, 2011.

For a briefer guide, see:

- Fowler, Simon. 'Assistant Poor Law Commissioners' Correspondence', in Thompson, K.M. *Short guides to records. Second series guides 25–48.* Historical Association, 1997, p.70–74.

Early correspondence of the Bradford Union is printed in:

• Carter, Paul, ed. *Bradford Poor Law Union: papers and correspondence with the Poor Law Commission October 1834–January 1839*. Yorkshire Archaeological Society Record Series 157. 2004.

The papers and correspondence of the assistant commissioners and inspectors who advised and supervised Boards of Guardians complement the papers in MH 12. These are in MH 32. They are, however, even more difficult to use for identifying specific paupers, although there are finding aids in MH 33. They are arranged by the names of the officers concerned. The correspondence between the Commission and Poor Law Inspectors in MH 9 is of a more general nature, although it may also be useful.

The Poor Law Commissioners' annual reports also contain a great deal of useful information, and frequently name individual paupers. The 1836 report, for example, contains a report on the 'Condition of Labourers who have migrated'. It includes very detailed accounts of individuals from Buckinghamshire who bettered themselves by moving north. The entry for James Hickman [illustrated], who moved from Princes Risborough to Stalybridge, even gives the names of his five children, as well as details of his occupations. Similarly, the 1843 report includes a list of paupers who were paid to work on the lunatic ward in St Peter's Hospital, Bristol.

STAYLEY BRIDGE.   Messrs. William Bayley & Brothers.

69. James Hickman, aged 32;. migrated with his wife and five children from Prince's Risborough. ·

He was a hawker, and earned 8s. per week. His wife had no employment. James, aged 12; Richard, aged 11; Suzy, aged 9; Thomas, aged 5; and George, aged 2, earned nothing.

He paid 1s. 6d. weekly for the rent of a cottage, containing three rooms, and much inferior to the cottage he now lives in.

He is now employed as a labourer, and earns 14s. His wife keeps house at home. James earns in the factory, 3s. 6d.; and Richard also, 3s. 6d., though their contract with Mr. Bayley was for 3s. per week.

Has three lodgers in his house, and receives 4s. 6d. towards his rent from them.

He pays 3s. 1d. weekly rent. Fuel is much cheaper here than in Buckinghamshire. He obtains better food, and more of it. Has written to advise a sister, who has a large family, to come; and he would recommend all labourers, with large families, to leave Buckinghamshire and come hither. The workpeople here behave very well to him; and his employers advanced money on his arrival to enable him to buy furniture, and have also advanced the wages of his two children. He would have come hither sooner had he known how much better this country was for a labouring man than Buckinghamshire.

Extract from the first Annual Report of the Poor Law Commission.

Further Reading

For an extensive guide to workhouses, see:

- Higginbotham, Peter. *The Workhouse encyclopedia*. History Press, 2012. Much of this is based on:
- The Workhouse
  www.workhouses.org.uk

The New Poor Law and the workhouse have attracted more than their fair share of studies. A still useful, if admittedly now dated, pamphlet summarising the varying views of different historians, is provided by:

- Digby, Anne. *The Poor Law in Nineteenth-Century England and Wales*. Historical Association G104. 1982.

For a useful collection of essays, see:

- Fraser, Derek, ed. *The New Poor law in the Nineteenth century*. Macmillan Press, 1976.

Good studies of the Workhouse include:

- Crowther, M.A. *The Workhouse System, 1834–1929: the history of an English social institution*. Methuen, 1983.
- Fowler, Simon. *Workhouse: the people, the places, the work behind doors*. National Archives, 2007.

This chapter has concentrated on those records in which the names of paupers can be found. There are a wide variety of other records, relating, for example, to staff, accommodation, and policy. For a detailed guide to all post-1834 poor law records, at both national and local levels, see:

- Carter, Paul. *A Guide to Records Created Under the New Poor Law*.
  http://my.balh.org.uk/education/BALH-Guide-to-Records-Created-Under-the-New-Poor-Law.pdf

See also:

- Reid, Andy. *The Union workhouse: a study guide for teachers and local historians*. Phillimore, for the British Association for Local History, 1994.

Numerous databases and digitised images of poor law records are online. Many – some of which have already been noted – are hosted by Find My Past **www.findmypast.co.uk** and Ancestry **www.ancestry. co.uk**. Family Search **www.familysearch.org** has Cheshire Workhouse Records 1848–1967, Kent Workhouse Records 1777–1911, and Norfolk Poor Law Union Records, 1796–1900.

For a full listing of over 14,000 long-term workhouse inmates, taken from a Parliamentary paper, see:

- England and Wales, Long-Term Workhouse Inmates, 1861 **https://search.ancestry.co.uk/search/db.aspx?dbid=61439** A partial free index to this list is also available at **www.genuki.org.uk/ big/eng/Paupers**

Irish poor who were removed from English unions in 1859–60 are listed by:

- Ireland, Poor Law Union Removals From England, 1859–1860 **https://search.ancestry.co.uk/search/db.aspx?dbid=61317**

For Cambridgeshire workhouses, see

- *The Cambridgeshire Union Workhouses Inmates Registers.* CD. Cambridgeshire Family History Society, nd.
- *Cambridge & Chesterton Workhouses Minutes 1836–1915...* CD. Cambridgeshire Family History Society, nd.

A number of workhouses have been turned into museums. These (especially Southwell) are well worth a visit to get a flavour of workhouse life, and some have small archival collections. See:

- The Workhouse: Visit a Workhouse Museum **www.workhouses.org.uk/visit**

Chapter 6

VAGRANTS

Poverty created both vagrants and paupers. The two words were frequently regarded by the authorities as almost synonymous. Paupers, that is, those who claimed poor relief, might be treated as if they were vagrants, and vice versa. The strict letter of the law, however, regarded them as two entirely separate categories. Admittedly, the tendency to conflate the two was greatly encouraged by the Vagrant Removal Cost Act, 1700. It placed the burden of removing vagrants on counties rather than on parishes, as hitherto. Parishes, however, still had to pay the costs of removing genuine paupers. The effect of the Act was to encourage overseers to treat paupers as vagrants in order to reduce their costs.[1] Indeed, it was claimed that overseers encouraged paupers to beg so that they could be arrested for vagrancy![2] That could be to the advantage of the pauper too: there was no appeal against vagrant removals, and effectively gave the vagrant settlement in the parish to which he was removed.[3] The objective of sixteenth-century vagrancy legislation was to remove vagrants to the parish of their birth, if that could be determined.[4]

Vagrants were greatly feared, and were a major issue for Justices of the Peace, overseers, and constables, for many centuries. The fear was, however, overblown. Court records reveal little sign of the large gangs of vagrants wandering the country and threatening its inhabitants described in preambles to Acts of Parliament and in popular literature. In practice, Justices had to deal primarily with individual vagrants who sometimes committed opportunistic crimes in order to survive.[5]

An Act of 1531 defined the vagrant as 'any man or woman whole and mighty in body and able to labour, having no land, master, nor using any lawful merchandise, craft or mystery whereby he might get his living'.[6] The landless poor were a new element in sixteenth-century society. Vagrants were poor, able-bodied men and women, without employment or fixed abode. They were rootless wanderers. In a society where everyone was required to have a master, they were masterless. Their defining characteristic was assumed to be idleness.

That assumption determined how vagrants were treated by the authorities.[7] They were regarded as lawless and dangerous. They were suspected of spreading corruption, and of breaking the accepted norms of society. Many were accused of deserting their wives and families. Servants and apprentices who absconded from their masters could be regarded as vagrants. So could prostitutes, although prostitution itself was not illegal. The vagrant's 'crime' derived from his status, rather than any act against a specific individual. In the sixteenth and seventeenth century, many vagrants were apprehended on the roads while travelling. A fifth of those apprehended stated their intended destinations. They were frequently headed for towns. In Wiltshire, most were travelling to Bath, Bristol, London or Salisbury.

Others were apprehended at fairs and markets. Such gatherings enabled them to cadge a living. The fair was a place for pedlars to hawk their wares, for creditors and debtors to settle accounts, for the workless to seek a master, and for thieves to exercise their craft.[8]

It is not possible to place an accurate figure on the number of vagrants. In the late seventeenth century, estimates ranged from 30,000 to 100,000.[9] In the early nineteenth century, numbers were increasing. Middlesex sent 540 vagrants to their parishes of settlement in 1808/9, but 6,689 in 1818/19.[10] In 1906, the Departmental Committee on Vagrancy estimated that there was a hard core of 20,000 to 30,000 permanent vagrants; if those tramping to seek work were added, there were perhaps 40,000 on tramp in good times, and 80,000 in bad times.[11]

The vagrant poor were predominantly urban in origin. Beier has calculated that, between 1516 and 1642, three-fifths of vagrants for whom examinations survive were 'settled' in towns. Urban life evidently tended to create the conditions which forced the poor into vagabondage.[12]

Youthful vagrants were a particular concern. In 1536, Richard Morison complained about the 'young and lusty, [who] neither have, nor yet will learn any honest occupation'.[13] When houses of correction were established in 1567, their chief purpose was 'that youth may be accustomed and brought up in labour and work'.[14] The law required child vagrants to be placed in service. A 1572 statute ordered them to be placed in the stocks or whipped. Youthful vagrants continued to be a problem into the nineteenth century. In 1803, it was estimated that three-fifths of beggars in London were children. Three years later, another estimate counted around 60,000 vagrants in England, of whom around

15,000 were aged under fifteen.[15] By the end of the nineteenth century, however, numbers had been drastically reduced, largely as a result of the rapid expansion of orphanages, and the introduction of compulsory schooling (especially the reformatory and industrial schools).[16]

Irish vagrants were another important group. 'Ireland prescribeth to be the nursery [of the Cornish poor]', according to Carew.[17] He wrote in around 1601, but the problem continued into the nineteenth century. In the seventeenth century, the Irish Sea was rather like the Mediterranean today. Many smugglers attempted to transport destitute Irish to England, despite the fact that it was illegal to do so. Conflict and distress in Ireland frequently resulted in increased migration – especially during the mid-seventeenth century rebellions, and during the Great Famine of the 1840s. The Westminster parish of St Mary le Strand paid doles to no fewer than eighty Irish in 1648–9.[18] The Guardians at Richmond (Surrey) relieved no fewer than ninety-nine Irish in the week ending 18 December 1847.[19]

In the nineteenth century, many Irish migrants were to be found working as navvies building railways. They moved around between construction sites. Others were harvest workers, who also moved around. They were not 'settled', and hence treated as vagrants. Many were removed by the authorities, and sent back to Ireland. For Irish paupers removed c.1859–60, see:

• Ireland, Poor Law Union Removals From England, 1859–1860
  https://search.ancestry.co.uk/search/db.aspx?dbid=61317

Gypsies were another concern. Like the Irish, they were regarded with much prejudice, and subjected to a separate body of legislation. The 1530 Egyptians Act required them to leave the country or suffer imprisonment. They were described as 'using no craft nor feat of merchandise', and 'going from place to place in great company and used great subtle and crafty means to deceive the people'. The statute remained in force until 1840, although a variety of other statutes dealing with the same issue were subsequently passed.[20] Nevertheless, penal legislation against gypsies was frequently not enforced.

Vagrants were greatly feared by the settled population. Indeed, even today children still remember that fear:

> Hark, hark, the dogs do bark
> The beggars are coming to town
> Some in rags, some in jags,
> And some – in velvet gowns!

While there are various interpretations of what we now regard as a nursery rhyme, the fact that it survives clearly reflects a real fear and distrust of itinerant beggars. The laws against them were harsh, and in some cases draconian; the Act of 1547 for example, prescribed branding and two years' enslavement for a first offence, and death for a second. In the eighteenth century, a third offence was still a felony, subject to the death penalty. The 1563 Statute of Artificers was a little less severe; it merely threatened imprisonment to any able-bodied labourer who refused to work in husbandry, or who deserted his master before his agreed term was complete. Under an Act of 1597, 'dangerous rogues' could be sent into exile, and some were transported.[21]

Despite such laws, however, the authorities sometimes complained that the common people did not have a 'right appreciation' of the crime of vagrancy, and thwarted attempts to stamp it out by ill-advised alms-giving.[22] Indeed, in 1757, the Middlesex Justices observed that it could sometimes be 'very dangerous for the Peace Officers to whip Sturdy Beggars'.[23] Passers-by were likely to be too sympathetic to the beggars. Consequently, whipping was increasingly inflicted in Houses of Correction, rather than on the streets.[24] In the late eighteenth century, the authorities in the City of London seem to have ceased the practice of whipping and sending vagrants to Bridewell; instead, they simply issued passes to convicted vagrants – or perhaps even issued them on request. The lack of punishment may have made obtaining a pass attractive to seasonal workers and others, who thus obtained free travel and medical treatment.[25]

Various Acts of Parliament required regular searches for vagrants to be made. Vagrancy figured largely in Charles I's 1631 'book of orders', which required Justices to undertake a variety of administrative tasks, and imposed detailed reporting requirements on them. That was probably because the tendency of constables was not to apply them rigorously. The extent to which the vagrancy laws were strictly applied is dubious. From the 1680s, Warwickshire Quarter Sessions regularly issued injunctions to put the vagrancy laws into full effect. They would not have needed to do so if constables had already been doing it. In fact, although no fewer than 6,004 migrants are recorded in the constables' accounts of Grandborough (Warwickshire), Hitchcock could only find evidence that one was punished.[26] In the eighteenth century, the management of vagrancy shifted from the parishes to the counties, and was separated from the administration of the poor law.[27]

The term 'vagrant' was frequently used imprecisely, at least until the Vagrant Act 1714, which defined the term more closely. Overseers frequently threatened migrants with charges of vagrancy, in order to move them on and ensure that they did not become a charge on the poor rates. Hence migrants could be forced to become vagrants, and the settlement provisions of the poor law sometimes had the perverse effect of exacerbating vagrancy.[28] For example, in 1680 Edward Conduit and his family were apprehended as vagrants in Warwick. Quarter Sessions determined that he had actually 'lived by his labour' in Arnesby (Leicestershire) for many years. They ordered him to be sent back to Arnesby; it seems likely that the overseers there had sought to exclude him when he needed poor relief.[29] Similarly, in 1734 the overseers of Horley (Surrey) gave Elizabeth Jones the substantial sum of five shillings 'to carry away Jane Jones her bastard child who was a little time before legally removed... from Newdigate in this county to Horley'.[30] Legally, she had nowhere else to go, but evidently took the money and left the parish, taking the risk of becoming a vagrant. Overseers' restrictive interpretations of the settlement laws meant that unmarried mothers, ex-soldiers, soldiers' wives, domestic servants who could not find work, and other unsupported women, were frequently forced into vagrancy.[31]

'Vagrant' frequently meant whatever a Justice of the Peace wished it to mean. The charge of vagrancy could be used against drunks, seducers, vandals, thieves, and even against those who slandered their neighbours. It was also used against a variety of dubious itinerant occupations: strolling players, minstrels, bear-wards, tinkers, itinerant (and frequently fraudulent) medics, wizards, and badgers – that is, pedlars. In eighteenth-century Westmorland, many vagrants were soldiers.[32] Minor crimes

A vagrant being whipped.

frequently resulted in a prosecution for vagrancy, since it was much simpler to prosecute: single Justices had summary jurisdiction, and no jury was required. The punishment for more serious crimes could be mitigated by prosecuting for vagrancy instead. Many Justices failed to follow the strict letter of the law, and avoided inflicting mutilation or whipping.

Not all itinerants were treated as vagrants. In fact, it has been estimated that convicted vagrants made up only 6% of the itinerant poor in the early seventeenth century.[33] The career of Bampfylde-Moor Carew, known as the 'king of the beggars', exemplifies the fact that, despite the law, vagrants were rarely apprehended. Despite his reputation, and the fact that he was well known, Carew spent thirty years roving and begging across the south-west, with occasional forays to Newfoundland, but was only prosecuted on a handful of occasions prior to his transportation to Maryland in 1739.[34]

Entertainers might be patronised by the nobility, or by borough corporations. Badgers could obtain licences.[35] Medics needed a licence from the bishop, although most of those who had them were not itinerant. Justices could license local beggars to beg in specific areas, and could grant passes to legitimate travellers, such as soldiers returning from wars, shipwrecked mariners, or poor students travelling to the universities. In the eighteenth century, passes could sometimes be had for the asking.[36] Even vagrants could be granted walking passes, which meant they were not accompanied by constables. Such passes were wide open to abuse. They could enable vagrants to wander around the country, rather than travelling to the place authorised by the issuing Justice. Effectively, they were licences to beg. As such, they were valuable documents. Despite the ease with which they could be obtained, they were frequently forged. Believable stories of losses by fire, enslavement by Barbary pirates, and shipwrecks at sea, are common among the forged passes found in Dorset Quarter Sessions papers.[37] These passes only survived because the forgeries were discovered. Until 1744 (see below), few other passes survive.

Vagrants were required to find masters. Many lists of 'masterless men' ordered to find masters are to be found among Quarter Sessions rolls. Conviction for vagrancy generally meant a whipping, perhaps mutilation of one's ear, and perhaps incarceration in a House of Correction, or in prison. The death penalty was infrequent, although it was inflicted; four vagrants were hanged at Middlesex sessions in 1575–6.[38] Punishment would normally be followed by removal to the parish of settlement, where poor relief would be payable. Alternatively, vagrants could be pressed to serve in the army or navy. In London, they were frequently sent to Bridewell (see below, p.157–8). Many were sent overseas as 'indentured servants'. Some of those sent from Bristol in the seventeenth century are listed in:

• Coldham, P.W. *The Bristol register of Servants sent to foreign plantations, 1654–1686.* Baltimore: Genealogical Publishing, 1988. For some similar publications, see below, p.144.

A variety of documents were created in the process of dealing with vagrancy, and can be used by family historians. Indeed, the whole system, especially after the 1714 Act, has been described as 'extremely bureaucratic', since it required documentation at almost every step.[39] Constables' accounts, where they survive, may record expenditure incurred in dealing with vagrants; for example, the Wigginton (Oxfordshire) constable in 1780 claimed one shilling for 'a journey to Banbury to satisfy the justice where I had taken an idle fellow for a souldier'.[40] Hundred constables and juries frequently presented vagrants to Quarter Sessions; their presentments are likely to be among Quarter Sessions rolls. Orders relating to them may be in Quarter Sessions order books.

The number of presentments mentioning vagrants declined in the late seventeenth and eighteenth century, as the process of examination by Justices of the Peace mandated by the 1662 Settlement Act increasingly took hold.[41] Vagrant examinations are very similar in format to the settlement examinations considered above (p.70–71). Indeed, record offices sometimes mis-classify them as settlement examinations.[42] They are however, a distinct category of document. They were used not only to determine the parish of settlement, but also to detect crime, specifically the crime of vagrancy.

The Vagrant Act 1714 required vagrant examinations to be written out in duplicate; one copy was to be lodged with the Clerk of the Peace, and may now be found either with the Sessions rolls, or in separate bundles. Justices also had to either write a warrant for committal to the House of Correction or prison, or issue a pass for the conveyance of the vagrant to the place of settlement. The Act, which consolidated all previous Acts, required Justices to deposit a duplicate of the passes they wrote with the Clerk of the Peace. The originals went with the vagrants. Sometimes, examinations, passes, and warrants were written on a single form. The examination may be annotated with the term of incarceration in the House of Correction, and signed by the vagrant as well as by the

Justice. The duplicate was sent with the escorting officer to the House of Correction or parish of settlement,[43] and may perhaps be found among either parish or Quarter Sessions records. The survival of both passes and examinations is of course dependent on the efficiency of the Justice who issued them; many failed to file them. It has been estimated that perhaps 30% of Cambridgeshire examinations survive; for Dorset the figure is 21%, and for Hampshire and Lancashire less than 10%.[44] The vagrant pass system was abolished by the Vagrancy Act 1824, except for dealing with Irish and Scottish vagrants.[45]

Registers of vagrants whipped and removed should have been kept by each parish, in accordance with a 1597 statute.[46] With a few exceptions these do not survive. The exceptions are mostly urban. The Salisbury register, for example, records that in April, 1598, 'William Coxe, an idle wandering rogue and sturdy beggar, was punished. Passport to Godishill in Fordingbridge, Hants, where he was born.'[47] Similar lists of vagrants were sent by Justices of the Peace to the Privy Council in the 1630s; these cover Devon and Cornwall, Lancashire and Westmorland, Kent, Sussex and Surrey, and Hertfordshire; they are in SP 16.[48]

The Vagrant Act 1700 made counties, rather than parishes, responsible for the cost of conveying vagrants to their places of settlement. Justices gave parish constables certificates specifying how many were to be conveyed, where they were to be taken, the mode of transport, and the allowances due to the constable. Constables returned this certificate to high constables, who claimed the allowance from the county treasurer.[49] From 1714, these certificates had to be produced to Quarter Sessions by the treasurer. Constables' claims listed vagrants conveyed, the routes used, and expenses such as subsistence costs for sick vagrants, burial and lying-in costs, horse hire, and charges for guards.

Some counties appointed contractors to undertake the work of removal; their claims for expenses were similarly detailed. In Middlesex, James Adams, and, later, his son Henry, regularly produced a list of vagabonds conveyed, indicating the bridewell or other place from whence he collected his passengers, the date of their pass, the place where they were delivered, their place of settlement, and the name of the magistrate who signed the pass. He also filled in blank certificates for each vagrant, giving their names and destinations, which had to be signed by the constable to whom he was handed over. These forms provided the evidence used by Adams to claim his subsistence money from the county treasurer.[50]

The terms 'vagrant' and 'casual' in the nineteenth century covered a wide range of cases, which did not fit neatly into official definitions.

Some were indeed the 'persons of
dissolute character' described by
the Poor Law Commissioners in
1841: they 'lead habitually a life
of laziness and imposture, and
not infrequently resort to violence
and intimidation'.[51] Rootless and
aimless tramps who rarely worked
could not, however, fairly be
compared with the van-dwelling
gypsies and tinkers who rarely
sought admittance to workhouses,
except in case of sickness. Nor could
they be compared with the many
thousand Londoners who travelled
into Kent during the hop-picking
season, and who used casual wards
as stopping off places on their way.

William Morrissey alias Smith, arrested for sleeping rough.

Then there were seamen travelling between ports seeking their next ship,
Irish seasonal labourers and victims of famine, and navvies moving from
construction site to construction site. For all of them, if they were caught
begging or sleeping rough, they risked a brief spell of hard labour under
the Vagrancy Act 1824.

The 1824 Act was Parliament's response to the changing nature
of vagrancy and its punishment. In the eighteenth century, corporal
punishment gradually ceased. Rather, vagrants were incarcerated in
houses of correction, where they were put to work. The Act provided
a thorough reformation of vagrancy law. It made sleeping rough and
begging criminal offences, punishable by up to one month's hard labour.
Recidivists – 'incorrigible rogues' – could still be flogged. In 1869, there
were 17,541 prosecutions for begging, and 5,323 for sleeping rough.[52]
The last flogging for begging took place in 1913. The offence of sleeping
rough was abolished in 1935, but the offence of begging is still on the
statute book. The 1824 Act also abolished the vagrant pass system,
except for vagrants from Ireland and Scotland. However, it authorised
passes for soldiers and sailors. Discharged prisoners could also obtain
passes for their journeys to parishes of settlement.

With the advent of 'less eligibility' in 1834, vagrants (frequently referred
to as 'casuals') posed a particular problem which was not dealt with by
the New Poor Law. Some Guardians assumed that, since they were not
mentioned, there was no need to relieve casuals. When some died after

being refused admittance to workhouses, the Poor Law Commissioners ordered Guardians to relieve all who applied, and to construct casual wards for vagrants. They might be cleaned up and given a bread and water supper. Their bed was often the floor, perhaps with some straw. In return for their night's lodging, they were usually required to undertake a piece of work, such as stone-breaking or oakum-picking, before being allowed to leave – with no breakfast – in the morning.[53] Some unions kept separate admission and discharge registers (see above, p.93–4) for casuals. In some counties, the newly formed police forces were given the task of issuing casual ward admission tickets. The Richmond (Surrey) Guardians offered a police officer £20 per annum to serve as a relieving officer for vagrants in 1864.[54] 'Way tickets' were given to those believed to be genuinely looking for work, and specified the route they had to take. Tickets gave them preferential treatment at specific destinations.

There were also a number of private initiatives to deal with the problem of nineteenth-century vagrancy. Mendicity societies enabled subscribers to issue vagrants with tickets which they could take to the societies' offices, where they would be interviewed, and, if found to be deserving, given food, a bed, and perhaps an emergency dole. Sometimes the records of these societies survive; for example, Lambeth Palace Library holds a number of late nineteenth-century reports on applicants to the Mendicity Society, together with a variety of related documents.

Vagrants remained a problem throughout the nineteenth and twentieth century. Many unions employed assistant relieving officers – frequently policemen – to deal with them.[55] The county police forces

Applicants for Admission to a Casual Ward.

created after 1839 monitored the number of vagrants passing through their jurisdiction.[56] In the years before 1914, between 5,000 and 12,000 vagrants were prosecuted for sleeping rough.[57] A 1929 inquiry suggested that perhaps a quarter of vagrants were suffering from mental problems.[58] It is likely that police archives include some material relating to vagrants, but they are not very fully catalogued at present.

Further Reading

Four books deal with vagrants in successive periods:

- Beier, A.L. *Masterless men: the Vagrancy problem in England 1560–1642.* Methuen, 1985.
- Hitchcock, David. *Vagrancy in English Culture and Society, 1650–1750.* Bloomsbury, 2016.
- Eccles, Audrey. *Vagrancy in law and practice under the Old Poor Law.* Ashgate, 2012.
- Rose, Lionel. *Rogues and Vagabonds: Vagrant Underworld in Britain 1815–1985.* Routledge, 1988.

An older history is provided by:

- Ribton-Turner, C.J. *A History of vagrants and Vagrancy, and Beggars and Begging.* Chapman and Hall, 1887. Digitised at **https://archive.org**

The Salisbury vagrants' register has been published; see:

- Slack, P., ed. *Poverty in early Stuart Salisbury.* Wiltshire Record Society, 31. 1975. Digitised at **www.wiltshirerecordsociety.org.uk/pdfs/wrs_v31.pdf**

For information on other vagrants passing through Wiltshire, drawn from vagrant examinations and passes, see:

- Church, Rosemary, & Cole, Jean, eds. *A Miscellany of British & Irish vagrants passing through Wiltshire.* 3 vols. Wiltshire Family History Society, 2000. v.1. 1785 (part of) to 1789. v.2. 1798 to 1796. v.3. Vagrant passes in the Wiltshire County Treasurers Finance Papers 1702–1705, 1708–1712, 1740–1742, 1774–1776.

For a detailed guide to sources for gypsies, see:

- Floate, Sharon Sillers. *My ancestors were gypsies.* 3rd ed. Society of Genealogists, 2010

If you have gypsy ancestors, you might want to join:

- Romany and Traveller Family History Society
  https://rtfhs.org.uk
  This page has links to a variety of relevant websites.

In order to place your gypsy ancestors in context, read:

- Cressy, David. *Gypsies: an English History.* Oxford University Press, 2018.

Chapter 7

CRIMINALS: THE PROCESS OF CONVICTION

Introduction: The System

The criminal law was normally applied, in the first instance, by a single Justice of the Peace. He could bind over suspects to appear at Quarter Sessions, or to keep the peace. As an individual Justice, he could order punishment for minor offences; for example, he could have vagrants whipped. For more serious matters he sat with other justices at Petty Sessions, and at Quarter Sessions. The most serious cases, especially capital offences, might be sent to Assizes. The powers granted to a single Justice, and to Petty Sessions, steadily increased during the eighteenth century.

A variety of other bodies also possessed criminal jurisdiction. In London and Middlesex, it was exercised in the Old Bailey (see below p.130–31); in Wales, offenders appeared before the Court of Great Sessions (see below, p.129–30). Many boroughs had their own courts. So did a variety of other institutions, such as the duchies of Lancaster and Cornwall. Moral crimes were dealt with in ecclesiastical courts. Cases could also be heard in the Westminster courts of King's Bench (for serious criminal cases), Requests (supposedly for poor men oppressed by corrupt officials), and Star Chamber (for riotous behaviour). The Privy Council sat at the summit of the judicial heirarchy.

Prosecution[1] before the nineteenth century was generally undertaken by victims. But that cost time and money. There were alternatives: restitution from the offender, arbitration by a Justice of the Peace, the dismissal of a pilfering servant. Or the matter could simply be dropped.

In the eighteenth and early nineteenth century, many victims joined together in associations for prosecuting offenders. There were perhaps 4,000 associations at the end of the eighteenth century. Numerous prosecutions were launched or supported by them. Official involvement in prosecution was rare until the mid-nineteenth century.

The nineteenth century witnessed the transition from a relatively informal system of justice, in which Justices of the Peace could apply the law as they saw fit individually, to a system in which they were greatly constrained, and had to apply uniformity and formality to all the cases which came before them. One of the consequences for researchers is that records began to be kept much more systematically.

Prosecution was gradually taken over by professional police forces, which began to operate in the early nineteenth century. The police were 'charged with the maintenance of public order and the control of society in the widest sense, [and] embarked upon an unceasing surveillance of all aspects of working-class-life', focusing particularly on the detection, prosecution, and, if possible, the prevention of crime. Most police stations kept registers of local criminals and suspects.

In 1879, the office of Director of Public Prosecutions was created. He began to undertake the prosecution of important and difficult cases, and offered advice to the police, to Justices' clerks, and to others who wished to commence proceedings. Quarter Sessions and Assizes continued to adjudicate until 1971, when they were abolished. They were replaced by the Crown Courts.

For a good general introduction to the history of crime and punishment, see:

- Briggs, John, et al. *Crime and punishment in England: an introductory history.* UCL Press, 1986.

The authoritative account up until 1800 is:

- Beattie, J.M. *Crime and the courts in England, 1660–1800.* Clarendon Press, 1986.

Shorter periods are dealt with by

- Sharpe, J.A. *Crime in Early Modern England 1550–1750.* 2nd ed. Longman, 1999.
- Emsley, Clive. *Crime and society in England 1750–1900.* 2nd ed. Longman, 1996.

The beginning researcher may find it useful to consult:

- Paley, Ruth. *Using Criminal Records.* Public Record Office, 2001.

A much more detailed introduction to the records of courts of law since 1800 is provided by:

- Cale, Michelle. *Law and Society: an Introduction to Sources for Criminal and Legal History from 1800*. PRO Publications, 1996.

Two useful online guides are produced by the National Archives:

- Criminals and Convicts
  www.nationalarchives.gov.uk/help-with-your-research/research-guides/criminals-and-convicts
- Courts of Law Records held in other Archives
  www.nationalarchives.gov.uk/help-with-your-research/research-guides/courts-of-law-records-held-in-other-archives

A useful guide to internet and other resources is provided by:

- Connected Histories: Crime and justice: a research guide
  www.connectedhistories.org/guide.aspx?a=1

Examples of numerous original sources, with useful commentary, are printed in:

- Hawkings, David T. *Criminal Ancestors: a guide to Historical Criminal Records*. Sutton Publishing, 1992.

Procedure

Before the nineteenth century, criminal trials usually began with a complaint to a Justice of the Peace, who would take depositions from the complainant and any witnesses. If the complainant could apprehend the offender, the suspect would be examined by the Justice. This examination offered the accused his best opportunity to refute the charges against him. The Justice might bind the offender to appear at the next Quarter Sessions, and send the recognizance, examination, and 'informations' of witnesses to the Clerk of the Peace. Alternatively, he could commit the offender to the county gaol to await trial. He did not necessarily attend the subsequent trial, which had to be prosecuted by the victim. Alternatively, the Justice might act as arbitrator, and persuade the complainant to drop the charge in return for compensation.

Trials at Quarter Sessions began either with indictments based on the gaol calendar, informations from Justices of the Peace, or presentments from either the Hundred Constable, the Hundred jury, the Grand Jury, or a Justice of the Peace. The Grand Jury decided whether cases should proceed to trial, and marked the documents with the terms *'billa vera'* (true bill) or *'ignoramus'* (we do not know) to record their decisions.

Cases were actually heard by petty juries selected by the sheriff. Several cases would be heard at once. Verdicts required juries to be unanimous. It was not until the eighteenth century that cases began to be heard separately, and not until the nineteenth century that the confrontation between accuser and accused became a confrontation between a prosecuting lawyer and a defence lawyer. The latter were not permitted until the mid-eighteenth century.

Documents

A wide variety of documents can be found among Quarter Sessions records held in county record offices. The court's responsibilities were wide-ranging, and not just concerned with criminal matters. It was the prime organ of county government until 1888, concerned with matters such as licensing alehouses, repairing bridges, and levying county rates. In the seventeenth and eighteenth century, many Quarter Sessions responsibilities were gradually devolved to local Petty Sessions. Their records are likely to be among Quarter Sessions records. From 1847, Clerks of Petty Sessions were required to make returns of all convictions of juvenile offenders to the Clerk of the Peace. Similar legislation in 1848 required them to make a return of all fines imposed, and, from 1855, they had to forward all depositions and case papers. These records may be informative.

A detailed guide to Quarter Sessions procedure, and to the records it produced, is provided by:

• Raymond, Stuart A. *Tracing your Ancestors in County Records: a Guide for Family & Local Historians.* Pen & Sword, 2016.

For a detailed list of Quarter Sessions records, with locations, see:

• Gibson, Jeremy. *Quarter Sessions records for family historians: a select list.* 5th ed. Family History Partnership, 2007.

Many other documents, including the records of Assizes, can be found in the National Archives. Class numbers of many of these are given below. Hawkings (see above, p.121) lists relevant National Archives documents. Many of these relate to the lives of convicts after conviction, and will be considered in Chapter 8. The various documents created in the process of prosecution and conviction are described below.

Examinations and Informations

Justices, when they examined accused persons and sent them for trial, recorded their examinations. They also recorded the 'informations' of witnesses. Examinations and informations provide many details of particular cases, sometimes including details of relationships. They are eyewitness accounts of events experienced by our ancestors centuries ago. For example, in 1648 John Freake of Stourton (Wiltshire) accused his servant Edith Courtney of stealing a gold ring and removing other valuables. The Justice who took Freake's 'Information' examined Edith, together with John Tabor, another suspect.[2] Both denied involvement. The Information and Examinations were found in the Sessions great rolls; they had evidently been sent to the Clerk of the Peace for adjudication by Quarter Sessions.

Recognizances

Recognizances were made by Justices at the same time as they conducted examinations. These were bonds, requiring those bound either to take a specified action, or to pay a heavy penalty. They were used to ensure that suspects attended court, but also had other uses. Neighbours in dispute might be required to keep the peace; assault might be punished by a bond requiring good behaviour. Witnesses might be bound to attend court and give evidence.

Recognizances recorded the name of the suspect, his parish, and his occupation, together with the names of two sureties. The amount of the bond was also stated. Occasionally, they provide interesting information on the reasons for binding. They were sent to Clerks of the Peace, with examinations where appropriate, and are frequently found rolled up in the Session's great rolls. In more recent centuries they were retained in separate files. Sometimes registers of them were kept.

Presentments

Trials could be initiated by the presentments of high constables, Hundred juries, Grand Juries, and individual Justices. Many concerned administrative matters such as defective stocks, bridges and roads in need of repair, and disputed rates, which are outside of the scope of this book. Others, however, reported matters such as the keeping of unlicensed alehouses, the harbouring of vagrants, the failure to attend church, and annoying the neighbours. The Wiltshire Grand Jury, for example, presented Thomas Stephens of Barford St Martin 'for selling of ale & beare without licence' in 1626.[3] The 1666 Mere Hundred jurors presented 'Dorothy Turner wife of James Turner she being abusive to her neighbours in language & behaviour'.[4]

In the eighteenth century Hundred juries and constables frequently reported *'omnia bene'* – all well – and gradually ceased to make presentments. Justices, however, continued to do so, especially on administrative matters. Early presentments, like recognizances, are likely to be rolled up with other documents in Sessions' rolls. Sometimes, later presentments may be recorded in process books.

Gaol Calendars and Criminal Registers

Justices could commit offenders to the county gaol, where they had to cool their heels until the cases against them were heard. Gaol calendars record the names of prisoners, with their offences, the name of the committing magistrate, the date of committal, and sometimes other information such as occupations and ages. They were compiled by the gaoler who brought the prisoners before the bench for trial. From the late eighteenth century, these calendars were frequently printed. Sometimes they are annotated with the sentence imposed. Both manuscript and printed calendars were frequently used as wrappers for Quarter Sessions great rolls. From the mid-nineteenth century, these calendars of prisoners were printed after trials, and record sentences. They were increasingly filed separately among Quarter Sessions records.

Gaol calendars from the Assize courts are filed among the ASSI classes in the National Archives. Sometimes they may also be found among Quarter Sessions records. Committals to the Old Bailey, and the Central Criminal Court, 1815–49, are recorded in HO 16. For printed calendars from Newgate, 1782–1853, see HO 77. Hawkings (above, p.121) gives a full listing of surviving calendars filed separately, with locations.

Between 1805 and 1892, annual criminal registers in HO 27 (and HO 26 for Middlesex 1791–1849) list all persons charged with indictable offences, recording verdicts, sentences, and (where appropriate) dates of execution. Additional information is given in the Middlesex registers prior to 1802. From 1834 until 1848, ages and the degree of literacy are stated. These registers have been digitised by both **www.ancestry.co.uk**, and **www.findmypast.co.uk**. Those for London and Middlesex have been digitised by London Lives **www.londonlives.com**.

A number of websites contain relevant information. See, for example:

- Newgate Calendars of Prisoners 1782–1931
  www.digitalpanopticon.org/Newgate_Calendars_of_Prisoners_1782-1931
  This site indexes the records in HO 77, together with some records from CRIM 9. See also **www.findmypast.co.uk**.

- Calendars of Prisoners: Devon Quarter Sessions, DRO – Devon QS32 and QS34
  www.genuki.org.uk/big/eng/DEV/CourtRecords/Prisoners
- City of York Calendars of Prisoners 1739–1851
  https://search.findmypast.co.uk/search-world-records/city-of-york-calendars-of-prisoners-1739-1851
- England and Wales Criminal Registers 1791–1892 [for London and Middlesex only]
  www.digitalpanopticon.org/England_and_Wales_Criminal_Registers_1791-1892

Indictments

Indictments, usually based on gaol calendars, give the names, parishes and occupations of the accused, dates and places of offences, names of victims if appropriate, the value of goods stolen, and the supposed intention of the accused. They were perhaps more formal statements of cases against the accused than presentments, but the dividing line between the two in criminal cases was narrow, if not obscure.[5] Indictments had to describe offences against specific statutes, or identify specific common law offences. They carefully followed the proper forms to make sure they were not thrown out for insufficiency. Otherwise, however, accuracy did not matter. Consequently, occupations are frequently given as 'labourer', and the accused's place of residence is liable to be given as the place where the offence was committed. Dates are not always accurate. The value of stolen goods mentioned in indictments was frequently downgraded so that the defendant could be tried on a non-capital charge. An obvious example of this is provided by the indictment of Joseph Stenson of Leeds, who in 1801 was accused, among other things, of stealing 500 shilling pieces valued at three pence![6]

Order Books and Sessions Rolls

At the end of each Sessions, the Clerk of the Peace wrote up minutes or order books. It should be possible to collate the information found in them with the documents used during the Sessions. These were bundled up into rolls and filed. The calendar of prisoners and the *nomina ministrorum* (the list of officials who should have been present) were frequently used as wrappers. Thus recognizances, indictments, presentments, examinations and informations can all be found in the rolls, as can various other documents, such as lists of licensees, petitions relating to cottages and other matters, and lists of jurors. In more recent centuries, separate files were created for some of these documents. Rolls can be very messy to handle, especially if the paper is crumbling and they are tied up with seventeenth-century string. Consequently, record offices have sometimes flattened them and bound them into books.

Many order books and sessions rolls have been published. A detailed list of such publications is provided elsewhere,[7] but see, for example:

Kent
Knafla, Louis A., ed. *Kent at law 1602: the county jurisdiction: Assizes and Sessions of the Peace*. HMSO, 1994.

Lancashire
Quintrell, B.W., ed. *Proceedings of the Lancashire Justices of the Peace at the sheriff's table during Assizes week, 1578–1694*. Record Society of Lancashire and Cheshire, 121. 1981.

Lincolnshire
Peyton, S.A., ed. *Minutes of proceedings in Quarter Sessions held for the Parts of Kesteven in the County of Lincoln, 1674–1695. Part 1*. Lincoln Record Society, 25. 1931.

Surrey
Powell, Dorothy L., & Jenkinson, Hilary, eds. *Surrey Quarter Sessions records: order book and sessions rolls, 1659–1661*. Surrey Record Society 13. 1934. Also published by Surrey County Council. Further vols. cover 1661–63, 1663–6, and 1666–8,

Wiltshire
Johnson, H.C., ed. *Wiltshire county records: minutes of proceedings in sessions, 1563 and 1574 to 1592*. Wiltshire Archaeological and Natural History Society Records Branch, 4. 1949.

Some interesting depositions have been digitised at:

• Court Depositions of South West England, 1500–1700
  http://humanities-research.exeter.ac.uk/womenswork/courtdepositions

Justicing Books
Justices of the Peace were encouraged to keep their own records of the cases which came before them out of sessions. Some cases did not proceed any further, so 'justicing books' may contain information not available elsewhere.

Justicing books were private documents, which are most likely to be found among family papers. One such notebook was compiled by Sir Richard Colt-Hoare of Stourton (Wiltshire). He recorded many cases of poaching; for example, on 20 February 1800 he recorded the 'information' of James Dorrington of Mere, who stated that 'he saw Edward Ford of Mere set three wires for the destruction of game'.[8] Over 300 miles to the north, the mid-eighteenth century notebook of Edmund Tew of Boldon (Co. Durham) records many instances where employers had failed to pay their servants, or to provide them with food.

A number of justicing books have been published;[9] see, for example:

Durham

Morgan, Gwenda, & Rushton, Peter, eds. *The Justicing notebook (1750–64) of Edmund Tew, rector of Boldon.* Surtees Society, 205. 2000.

Middlesex

Paley, R. ed. *Justice in eighteenth century Hackney: the justicing notebook of Henry Norris and the Hackney petty sessions book.* London Record Society Publications, 28. 1991.

Wiltshire

Crittall, Elizabeth, ed. *The justicing notebook of William Hunt, 1744–1749.* Wiltshire Record Society, 37. 1982.

Assize Records

The Assize judges generally tried the more serious cases; that is, those for which the death penalty could be imposed. They also heard appeals against Quarter Sessions verdicts, including many relating to settlement. England (and, from 1830, Wales) was divided into circuits, each of which was the responsibility of particular judges drawn from the central courts who itinerated around them. Their records are very similar to those of Quarter Sessions. Records from 1558 to 1971 are in the National Archives ASSI classes. For Cheshire see CHES classes, for Durham see DURH classes. For Wales, see below, p.129–30.

The Crown minute, gaol, and agenda books list the accused and summarise cases heard. Pleas, verdicts and sentences are frequently noted. Similarly, Assize indictments formally record the charges against the accused, and are usually annotated with plea, verdict, and sentence. Witness statements and case papers provide much personal detail, especially for the more serious crimes of the nineteenth century. Depositions from the Assize circuits can be searched by the name of the accused at **http://discovery.nationalarchives.gov.uk**.

Before those convicted were sentenced, they could make the archaic plea for 'benefit of clergy'. This plea, in medieval times, had transferred sentencing to the ecclesiastical courts, where the death penalty could not be imposed. At that time, only the clergy were literate. They could therefore prove their clerical status, and thus their right to be sentenced in ecclesiastical courts (where the death penalty could not be imposed), by demonstrating their literacy. In subsequent centuries, the law failed to keep up with the spread of literacy, and it became a legal fiction that only the clergy were literate. Anyone who could read could plead 'benefit of clergy'. The right to make this plea was gradually eroded by Parliament, but it was not until the 1820s that benefit of clergy was finally abolished. Returns of those granted 'clergy'

REPORT OF

PROCEEDINGS

UNDER COMMISSIONS OF
Gt. Exit. Courts of general
Oyer & Terminer and Gaol Delivery,

FOR THE COUNTY OF

YORK,

HELD AT THE CASTLE OF YORK,

BEFORE

SIR ALEXANDER THOMSON, KNIGHT,
ONE OF THE BARONS OF THE EXCHEQUER;

AND

SIR SIMON LE BLANC, KNIGHT,
ONE OF THE JUSTICES OF THE COURT OF KING'S BENCH;

from the 2ᵈ to the 12ᵗʰ of January
1813.

FROM THE SHORT HAND NOTES OF MR. GURNEY.

To which are subjoined
TWO PROCLAMATIONS,
Issued in consequence of the result of those Proceedings.

London:
PRINTED BY LUKE HANSARD & SONS,
NEAR LINCOLN'S-INN FIELDS.

Report of Assize Proceedings at York.

at Assizes between 1518 and 1660 were made to King's Bench. Many of these returns were abstracted on the Controlment Rolls 1558–1625 (KB 29/192-273). A few returns survive in KB 9.

Information concerning convictions at Assizes can also be found by consulting Assize vouchers and sheriffs' cravings. Assize vouchers are lists of prisoners convicted at Assizes. Sheriffs' cravings are claims from sheriffs for maintaining prisoners prior to trial, for expenses at Assizes and at executions, and for conveying those sentenced to transportation to prison hulks. Both vouchers and cravings are held in class E 389 (1714 to 1832). Cravings are also in T 64 (1745–1785), E 197/32-4 (1722–1806), T 90 (1733–1822) and T 207 (1823–1959). Treasury warrants record, among other items, payments made to sheriffs to cover expenses incurred in apprehending and convicting criminals. They are in classes T 53 (1721–1805) and T 54 (1806–27). The books are indexed; indexes should be searched under the heading 'sheriffs' conviction money'.

For a guide to criminal records from the Assizes, see:

- Criminal trials in the Assize Courts 1559–1971
  www.nationalarchives.gov.uk/help-with-your-research/research-guides/criminal-trials-assize-courts-1559-1971

The best approach to finding relevant material is to consult:

- Criminal trials in the English Assize Courts 1559–1971
  www.nationalarchives.gov.uk/help-with-your-research/research-guides/criminal-trials-assize-courts-1559-1971

For Wales, which adopted the Assize system in 1830 (see below for earlier), see:

- Criminal and civil trials in the Welsh assize courts 1831–1971 – key to records
  www.nationalarchives.gov.uk/help-with-your-research/research-guides/criminal-civil-trials-welsh-assize-courts-1831-1971-key-to-records

Most surviving Elizabethan and early Stuart Assize records are in print, many edited by J.S. Cockburn. There are too many to give a full listing here, but see, for example:

- Cockburn, J.S., ed. *Calendar of Assize records: Home Circuit Indictments, Elizabeth I and James I. Introduction.* HMSO, 1985. Other volumes in this series cover Essex, Hertfordshire, Kent, Surrey, and Sussex.
- Cockburn, J.S., ed. *Western Circuit Assize orders, 1629–1648: a Calendar.* Camden 4th series, 17. Royal Historical Society, 1976.
- Barnes, T.G., ed. *Somerset Assize orders 1629–1640.* Somerset Record Society, 65. 1959. A further volume edited by Cockburn covers 1640–59.

For some nineteenth-century calendars, see:

- Johnson, D.A., ed. *Staffordshire Assize calendars, 1842–1843.* Collections for a History of Staffordshire 4th series, 15. 1992.

Court of Great Sessions
In Wales, the Court of Great Sessions was the equivalent of the Assizes between 1547 and and 1830. Its gaol files are the principal records of its criminal work, and include similar information to Quarter Sessions rolls,

especially indictments and gaol calendars. There are also numerous examinations, depositions, recognizances, presentments, and other documents. Criminal records from the Court are held by the National Library of Wales, and are listed by Hawkings (above, p.121). They are briefly described in:

- The Court of Great Sessions in Wales 1547–1830
  www.earlymodernweb.org.uk/waleslaw/gfintro.htm

For more detailed discussion, see:

- Parry, Glyn. *Guide to the records of Great Sessions in Wales.* Aberystwyth: National Library of Wales, 1995.

Old Bailey Proceedings

In London, courts of Quarter Sessions and Assizes did not sit. Instead, courts staffed by the Lord Mayor, recorder, and aldermen of London, together with King's Bench judges, sat at the Old Bailey, or sometimes at Guildhall. This arrangement ceased when the Central Criminal Court was established in 1834.

Trials at the Old Bailey were regularly reported under semi-official auspices. At first, reports were brief summaries, but they eventually became detailed transcripts of trials. They begin with the names of defendants and the charges against them, followed by testimonies from prosecution and defence witnesses. Juries' verdicts are then given, and reports are concluded by the ages of those found guilty, and sentences of the court (which were not necessarily implemented).

These printed *Proceedings* are in the National Archives, Class PCOM 1, in London Metropolitan Archives, and sometimes in other major research libraries. They can be read online at:

- The Proceedings of the Old Bailey, 1674–1913
  www.oldbaileyonline.org/index.jsp
  This includes a page on 'The Value of the Proceedings as a Historical Source', **www.oldbaileyonline.org/static/Value.jsp** which all users should read.

For a database of associated records, including pre-trial examinations and depositions, recognizances and bail records, and prosecution papers, as well as some pamphlet literature, see:

- Digital Panopticon: Old Bailey Proceedings 1740–1913
  www.digitalpanopticon.org/Old_Bailey_Proceedings_1740-1913

Genealogists rarely note that many other records of the Old Bailey prior to 1834 are held by London Metropolitan Archives. These and other court records from London and Middlesex may have additional information, and are described by:

- A Brief Guide to the Middlesex Sessions Records
  www.cityoflondon.gov.uk/things-to-do/london-metropolitan-archives/visitor-information/Documents/39-a-brief-guide-to-the-middlesex-sessions-records.pdf

See also:

- Sessions Records for the City of London and Southwark
  www.cityoflondon.gov.uk/things-to-do/london-metropolitan-archives/visitor-information/Documents/40-sessions-records-for-the-city-of-london-and-southwark.pdf

Indictments in the Central Criminal Court at the Old Bailey, 1834–1971, can be consulted in the National Archives, class CRIM 4. They are indexed in CRIM 5. Indictments commenced criminal proceedings, and give details of the offence, the plea, and the verdict. They also give residences, which may not appear in the *Proceedings*. CRIM 1 consists of depositions in cases of murder, sedition, riot, and other high-profile crimes, together with a 2% random sample of cases of supposedly lesser interest.

A very select number of depositions are in CRIM 1. Court books, 1834–1949, which summarise trials, and include details of offences, pleas, verdicts, sentences, the names of jurors, and perhaps the names of victims, are in CRIM 6. Minutes of evidence, 1834–1912, written in shorthand, and presumably forming the basis for the published *Proceedings*, are in CRIM 10.

For a useful guide to Old Bailey records, see:

- Trials in the Old Bailey and the Central Criminal Court
  www.nationalarchives.gov.uk/help-with-your-research/research-guides/trials-old-bailey-central-criminal-court

Police Records

Every policeman kept a notebook recording incidents that took place on his beat. Every police station kept an occurrence book. Where these survive, they provide much information on criminals, and indicate when proceedings in particular cases began. Charge books record the names of persons charged, with details of their offences. Metropolitan Police records are in the National Archives MEPO classes. These include various registers of criminals from 1834 in MEPO 6; and registers of murders and death by violence since 1891 are in MEPO 20. The daily reports from Metropolitan Police offices in HO 62, 1828–39, include much information regarding offenders and stolen property.

Police records in the provinces have sometimes been deposited in local record offices, but may still be in the hands of the police themselves, or perhaps in museums created by local forces. For a detailed guide to police archives, see:

- A Guide to the Archives of the Police Forces of England and Wales, Ian Bridgeman and Clive Emsley
  www.open.ac.uk/arts/research/policing/sites/www.open.ac.uk.arts. research.policing/files/files/ecms/arts-policing-pr/web-content/ guide-to-police-archives.pdf

Director of Public Prosecutions

From 1884, the Director of Public Prosecutions kept a register of the applications he received for advice on criminal prosecutions. Each volume is indexed by the accused, as well as by the applicant, and by the offence. Action was frequently not taken, but when it was the relevant court is noted. There are separate registers of miscellaneous papers 1899–1946, and of criminal appeals, 1908–33. These registers are in DPP 3.

There are also separate registers of prosecutions, 1905–86, undertaken at the Central Criminal Court in the Old Bailey. These are in DPP 9. They record the name of the accused, the offence, and the date, among other information.

For cases prosecuted by the Director, case files are in DPP 1 (1889–1930) and DPP 2 (1931–2012). These include copies of depositions and exhibits, counsel's briefs and papers, and correspondence.

Note that some of these files may be subject to closure for thirty or 100 years.

The Public Hue and Cry

In 1772, John Fielding, chief magistrate at Bow Street, began publishing *The Public Hue and Cry* (now known as the *Police Gazette*), which carried details of known criminals submitted by magistrates throughout the country. In 1831, it was said to contain the 'substance of all Informations received in Cases of Felonies, and Misdemeanors of an aggravated nature, and against Receivers of Stolen Goods, reputed Thieves and Offenders escaped from Custody, with the time, the place, and every particular circumstance marking the Offence', together with much other information. Many issues are available at the British Newspaper Archive **www.britishnewspaperarchive.co.uk**. Copies can also be read at LCTR: Last Chance to Read **www.lastchancetoread.com**, and at Ancestry **https://search.ancestry.co.uk/search/db.aspx?dbid=60861**. Research libraries and local record offices occasionally hold hard copies. There is a set in the National Archives, 1828–45, class HO 75.

Charles Booth

Charles Booth's investigations of the London poor led him and his collaborators to compile notebooks recording their activities accompanying police on their beats. These are available online:

- Charles Booth's London: Police Notebooks
  https://booth.lse.ac.uk/notebooks/police-notebooks

Ecclesiastical Courts

Until the nineteenth century, the ecclesiastical courts had jurisdiction over 'sin, sex and probate', as one author has put it. The poor were frequently accused of moral failings such as adultery, bastardy (as we have already seen), prostitution, and defamation. A variety of other topics were also dealt with, for example, recusancy, tithe, and probate, but these are outside of the scope of this book.

Every diocese had a Consistory court under its bishop. Most also had archdeaconry courts under archdeacons. Bishops and archdeacons usually appointed surrogates to sit on their behalf. There were also a range of peculiar courts; that is, courts for areas which were outside the normal jurisdiction of the diocesan bishop. The Provinces of Canterbury and York both had their provincial courts. The jurisdiction of ecclesiastical and secular courts frequently overlapped; indeed, occasionally the same case was heard in both.

Procedure in ecclesiastical courts frequently began with a churchwarden's presentment during visitation. Dioceses and archdeacons were regularly 'visited' by their superiors to make sure that all was in order. Churchwardens were expected to present at visitation any matters which they thought merited action by ecclesiastical judges. Many presentments survive, and reveal the concerns of parish officers.

They frequently describe offences such as drunkenness, misbehaviour in church, and fornication.

Procedure could also commence as the result of a citation to attend court. Many citations listing those summoned survive. Act books record proceedings and sentences. The depositions of witnesses provide us with eyewitness accounts of daily life in earlier centuries.

The punishments available to ecclesiastical judges were not severe. They could impose penance, or sentence the offender to excommunication. Penance usually involved the humiliation of appearing in the penitent's local church in a white sheet, and reading a confession. Excommunication was originally more serious; it theoretically prevented the excommunicate from having anything to do with anyone else. But in practice it was increasingly ignored, especially by Nonconformists and Roman Catholics (who did not regard themselves as members of the Church of England anyway).

Diocesan archives include presentments and other visitation records, citations, act books, and orders to local ministers to supervise confessions. Citations and orders were usually returned to the court once they had been acted upon.

For a detailed guide to the records of church courts, see Chapter 7 of:

- Raymond, Stuart A. *Tracing your Church of England Ancestors: a Guide for Family and Local Historians.* Pen & Sword, 2017.

More extensive guides are provided by:

- Tarver, Anne. *Church Court Records: an Introduction for Family and Local Historians.* Phillimore, 2015.
- Chapman, Colin. *Sin, sex and probate: Ecclesiastical Courts, Officials, & Records.* 2nd ed. updated. Lochin Publishing, 2009.

Thousands of depositions have been digitised by:

- Cause Papers in the Diocesan Courts of the Archbishop of York, 1300–1858
  www.dhi.ac.uk/causepapers

British Trials
Detailed reports of thousands of trials on charges such as murder and adultery, libel and treason, are included in a substantial microfiche collection held in major reference libraries:

- *British Trials 1660–1900.* 2,372 fiche + printed guide. Chadwyck-Healey, 1991.

Chapter 8

CRIMINALS: SENTENCING AND AFTER

Introduction

During the early modern period, felonies were punishable by death. Less serious crime might attract a whipping or a fine. Imprisonment was rare, although those convicted might be sent to Bridewell (see p.157–8), or to one of the Houses of Correction which began to be erected at the end of the sixteenth century. Punishment was at the discretion of the court, and there was a growing trend to reprieve those sentenced to death. Between 1825 and 1834 only 5% of those sentenced to capital punishment were actually executed.[1] Most were transported instead.

Transportation as a punishment was authorised by a 1597 Act, although it was little used until the Transportation Act 1718 provided central funding. Until the American War of Independence broke out in 1775, convicts were sent to North America. Thereafter, they were left languishing in hulks in the Thames, until Governor Philip founded a convict colony in New South Wales in 1788. Even then, many still served out their sentences in them. Almost two-thirds of those sentenced to transportation at the Old Bailey before 1775 had been sent to America; of those sentenced after 1788, only one-third actually went to Australia.[2]

The development of transportation as a punishment was paralleled by a variety of other changes to the nature of punishments available to Justices of the Peace and Assize judges. Physical punishments such as whipping and the pillory steadily lost favour. Greater emphasis was placed on imprisonment. The purpose of punishment was increasingly seen to be reformation, rather than merely punishment. Depraved minds had to be reformed by work, solitude, and religious instruction. That could not be done in the old county gaols. Their purpose was purely custodial; there was no concept of using them to reform behaviour. A

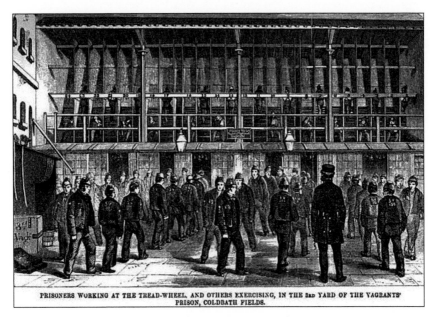

PRISONERS WORKING AT THE TREAD-WHEEL, AND OTHERS EXERCISING, IN THE 3rd YARD OF THE VAGRANTS' PRISON, COLDBATH FIELDS.

The exercise yard at Coldbath Fields Prison, showing tread wheels.

new type of institution was required: the prison. Many were built in the years following the Gaols Act 1784; a second wave of construction developed in the 1820s. They were designed so that silence, work, and sometimes solitary confinement could easily be enforced. By the mid-1850s, prisoners' lives were carefully regulated. Responsibility for prisons was gradually transferred from local to central government; by 1877, they were entirely under the control of Whitehall. Consequently, many sources for identifying prisoners in the nineteenth and twentieth century are in the National Archives.

Quarter Sessions and Assize Records

The prime focus of Quarter Sessions and Assize records is on the process of conviction, rather than on sentencing and imprisonment. We have, however, already seen that their order books and minutes recorded verdicts and sentences imposed, and that sometimes records such as indictments and gaol calendars, were annotated with these details. An order book from Somerset, for example, notes that, in 1621, Joan Clarke, the mother of a bastard child, was ordered 'to be brought to the next market town, and there to be stripped from the neck to the girdle and openly whipped'.[3]

The sentences imposed at Assizes were subject to the discretion of the Home Secretary, who exercised the Crown's prerogative of mercy.

From the end of the seventeenth century, Assize judges compiled 'circuit pardons' or 'circuit letters' at the end of each Assize, listing convicts they recommended for pardon. From 1728, they compiled separate lists of those they wanted transported or absolutely pardoned. These 'circuit letters' and lists are to be found in many ASSI and SP classes in The National Archives. In the South Eastern Circuit, Crown entry books, also known as agenda books (ASSI 31), constitute the best source for reprieves and pardons; they commence in 1748. Judges' reports on criminals, 1784–1830 (HO 47) were written by trial judges in response to petitions from convicts for clemency. The petitions themselves are in HO 17–19. Both of these sources include details of family circumstances, and both have been digitised (at least in part) by:

- England & Wales, Crime, Prisons & Punishment, 1770–1935
  https://search.findmypast.co.uk/search-world-records/england-and-wales-crime-prisons-and-punishment-1770-1935

For reports from the Recorder of London and other Old Bailey judges, see:

- Judges' Reports on Criminals 1784–1827
  www.digitalpanopticon.org/Judges_Reports_on_Criminals_1784-1827.

For an interesting study based on these sources, see:

- Eatwell, Alison. *Crime, Clemency and Consequence in Britain 1821–1839: a slice of criminal life*. Pen & Sword, 2017.

For pardons actually granted, see below, pp.142–3.

Police Records: the Habitual Criminals Register

After 1869, the Metropolitan Police maintained a register of habitual criminals, listing men discharged or about to be discharged from prison.[4] The register includes names and aliases of each offender, conviction and sentence details, and information on previous convictions. Detailed physical descriptions, including photographs, are also given. Updates were issued weekly to provincial police forces, and may sometimes be found locally. The main register is now in The National Archives, class MEPO 6, and has been digitised at:

- Metropolitan Police Register of Habitual Criminals 1881–1925
  **www.digitalpanopticon.org/Metropolitan_Police_Register_of_
  Habitual_Criminals_1881-1925**

Find My Past also has a database of the register, which also includes some entries from the *Police Gazette*, up until 1936, together with the register of habitual drunkards maintained by the Metropolitan Police 1903–14 (the original is in MEPO 6/77-88). Over 100,000 names, 1881–1936, are listed by:

- Metropolitan Police: Habitual Criminals and other Miscellaneous Papers
  **www.findmypast.co.uk/articles/world-records/full-list-of-united-
  kingdom-records/institutions-and-organisations/england-and-
  wales-crime-prisons-and-punishment-1770-1935/metropolitan-
  police-habitual-criminals-and-miscellaneous-papers**

Some forces created their own more detailed registers. The Birkenhead Register of Offenders, for example, runs from 1875 until 1938.[5]

Prison Registers and Records

The earliest gaol calendars were lists of those accused of crimes, rather than of those convicted. These were discussed in the previous chapter. The discussion here will primarily focus on convicted prisoners, although the records of the Prison Commissioners do include (in PCOM 2) a variety of calendars of prisoners awaiting trial at Quarter Sessions and Assizes, as well as many prison registers. The survival of these documents is fairly random.

PCOM 2 is a very diverse class, ranging in date from 1770 to 1951, and including registers from a wide range of prisons in England, as well as in Gibraltar. Pentonville, Chatham, Portsmouth, Millbank, and Wormwood Scrubs are particularly well documented. Also included are prison minute books, visitors' books, order books, journals of governors, chaplains and surgeons, and other documentation.

Class HO 24 consists of registers of convicts in the new prisons at Millbank, Parkhurst, and Pentonville, 1838–75. These include convicts' ages, marital status, number of children, and whether they were literate. The place and date of conviction, the crime, the sentence, previous offences, and details of movements within the prison system, are also recorded. On 7 October 1853, for example, the register of Millbank Prison records that Samuel Hawkins, widower, aged thirty-five, a sweep, had been convicted of felony at Oxford City Sessions. His 'character and connexions [were] bad', although he could read. He was sent to Van Diemans Land in the

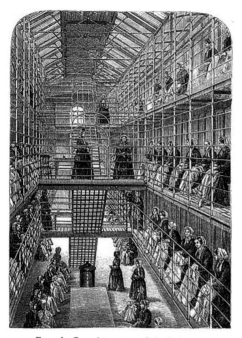

Female Convicts at work in Brixton Women's Prison, 1862.

Lincoln Prison (now a museum).

following January.[6] Similar registers in HO 23 give details of convicts in overflow prisons at Aylesbury, Bath, Leeds, Leicester, Northampton, Nottingham, Preston, Reading, Somerset, and Wakefield.

Printed registers of prisoners, 1868–1971, are in HO 140. They include the following information: number, name, age, trade, previous convictions, and details of the crime and conviction (including names of victims). Over 640,000 names are listed. For the Central Criminal Court at the Old Bailey, post-trial calendars of prisoners, 1855–1949, are in CRIM 9. All of the classes mentioned in this and the two preceding paragraphs are searchable at **www.findmypast.co.uk**, although not all have yet been completely digitised.

Prison records are sometimes held in local record offices. For example, the Plymouth Prison Records 1832–1919, digitised at **https://search. findmypast.co.uk/search-world-records/devon-plymouth-prison- records-1832-1919**, are held by Plymouth & West Devon Record Office.

From 1853, convicts could be paroled. Records of over 40,000 licences, 1853–87 are preserved in PCOM 3–4, and are digitised at **www. findmypast.co.uk**. Licences for female prisoners have also been digitised by **www.ancestry.co.uk**.The records include much information, noting, for instance, marital status, children, profession, and a full physical description. Photographs are included in more recent files. The registers of licences 1853–1949 in PCOM 6 provide indexes to PCOM 3–4. They also index the Captions in PCOM 5. These are copies of court orders relating to the imprisonment or transportation of convicts, together with transfer papers for removal to a prison; each caption includes penal records and other details of the prisoner concerned. Many papers relating to individual convicts 1876–1958 are in PCOM 8. Some other PCOM classes include similar material.

Personal files for convicts sentenced to death but reprieved, 1936–2005, are in HO 336. These provide comprehensive records of the lives of those convicted while in prison, detailing matters such as their conduct, medical and vocational training reports, and licences for early release. They also include photographs taken on reception and on release.

There are numerous other documents relating to prisons in both local record offices and The National Archives. Governors' journals, surgeons' orders, visitors' books, chaplains' journals, letter books, and a wide range of other documents can be found by the assiduous researcher. These all shed light on prison regimes, and frequently refer to individual prisoners. A comprehensive listing of nineteenth-century prison records, together with an extensive *Guide to the Criminal Prisons of Nineteenth-Century England*, is provided by:

• Prison History
  www.prisonhistory.org

A variety of registers and other records for Gloucestershire have been digitised by Ancestry:

• Gloucestershire, England, Prison Records, 1728–1914
  https://search.ancestry.co.uk/search/db.aspx?dbid=60895

Ancestry also has databases of various records from Bedfordshire Gaol, 1770–1882, Bodmin Gaol 1821–99, Dorchester Prison, 1782–1901, Swansea and West Glamorgan prisons, 1870–1922, and Wakefield Prison 1801–1914.

A particularly interesting source is provided by photographs of prisoners at Wandsworth Prison (PCOM 2/290-1). These can be searched at:

• Victorian prisoners' photograph albums 1872–1873
  www.nationalarchives.gov.uk/help-with-your-research/research-guides/victorian-prisoners-photograph-albums-1872-1873

For a useful introduction to searching for particular prisoners, see:

- Prisoners and prison staff
  www.nationalarchives.gov.uk/help-with-your-research/research-guides/prisoners-or-prison-staff

See also:

- Hawkings, David T. 'Prison Registers and Prison Hulk Records', in Thompson, K.M., ed. *Short Guides to Records Second Series 25–48*. Historical Association, 1997, p.123–6.

For the history of prisons, see:

- Potter, Harry. *Shades of the Prison House: A History of Incarceration in the British Isles*. Boydell Press, 2019.

Juvenile Delinquency

Young offenders have always been responsible for a high proportion of criminal acts.[7] Early attempts to reform juvenile delinquents were made by a number of charities (including the Marine Society, mentioned

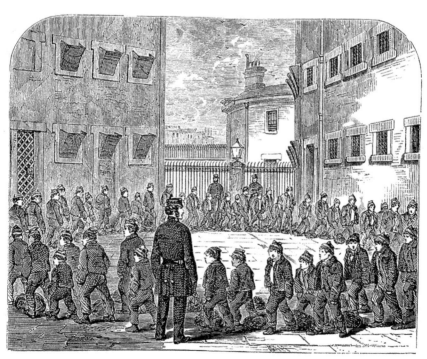

Boys Exercising at Tothill Fields. Courtesy Wellcome Collection.

above, p.58). The first permanent government establishment for dealing with them was Parkhurst Prison, opened in 1835, which catered for boys until 1868. Registers are in the National Archives, class HO 24/15.

The Youthful Offenders Act 1854 created reformatory schools, intended for children under sixteen convicted of crimes. These were privately run; by 1875 fifty-four had been opened. They should not be confused with certified industrial schools, which were intended for children under fourteen thought to be in danger of falling into crime. A variety of registers, log books, and related documents from both types of school are in HO 329.

Borstals were intended for youths between the ages of sixteen and twenty-one. They aimed to separate youths from older offenders, and provided a regime which was educational rather than punitive, although it was highly regulated. Routine, discipline and authority were emphasised, especially in the early years. They derived their name from the village in Kent where one of the first Borstals was opened in 1902. The Prevention of Crime Act 1908 formalised the system, and many 'Borstals' were built. Registers of Borstal inmates 1905–77, together with details of after-care provisions, a random sample of personal files, and other documents, are in HO 247.

Home Office Papers
When the Home Office was established in 1782, it began to keep entry books solely devoted to its correspondence on criminal matters. These are in HO 13 for 1782–1871. Before 1849, they include warrants for the transfer of convicts between prisons, or into the army or the navy. They also include warrants for pardons and reprieves. Entry books can be searched at:

- Home Office Criminal Entry Books 1782–1876
  www.digitalpanopticon.org/Home_Office_Criminal_Entry_Books_1782-1876

Correspondence and other papers relating to criminals, 1849–71, are in HO 12, and registered in HO 14. For in-letters, 1820–43, relating to prisons and convict ships, and including papers relating to criminal lunatics at Bethlem, see HO 20. Out-letters 1812–84 are in HO 21. Another series of out-letters, running from 1899–1921 is in HO 163. For the main series of Home Office letters and papers, see HO 45.

The criminal warrants entered in HO 13 prior to 1849 are continued in HO 15 from 1850, and in HO 147 from 1887 until 1921. Draft letters patent granting pardons for 1802–80 are in C 197/28. Class HO 188 includes warrants for pardoning convicted criminals and remitting sentences, 1887–1960.

Letters to the Bank of England

In 1797, gold was withdrawn as a currency, and replaced by paper notes issued by the Bank of England. These were of poor quality, and easy to forge. The forgers got busy; in the following two decades some 2,000 offenders were prosecuted. At the Old Bailey, between 1804 and 1834, the Bank's solicitors procured 126 death sentences, and 565 sentences of transportation. Most death sentences were respited, but most sentences of transportation were carried out. At least 425 of the convicted wrote to the Bank appealing for mercy. Their letters give many interesting details of family life, and are still in the Bank's archives. They have been edited in:

• Palk, Deirdre, ed. *Prisoners letters to the Bank of England 1781–1827.* London Record Society 42. 2007.

Transportation

Records of those sentenced to transportation are to be found among both Quarter Sessions and Assize records. Some 50,000 convicted felons were transported to North America before independence in 1776.[8] Australia received at least 160,000 between 1787 and 1867. In the eighteenth century, the names of transportees were recorded in transportation bonds. These were entered into by contractors who undertook the task of transportation, and are frequently to be found amongst Quarter Sessions records. Transportation contracts for Middlesex are digitised at:

• Middlesex, England, Convict Transportation Contracts, 1682–1787 **https://search.ancestry.co.uk/search/db.aspx?dbid=2381**

For various Dorset records, see:

• Dorset, England, Convict Transportation Records, 1724–1791 **https://search.ancestry.co.uk/search/db.aspx?dbid=2214**

Among Assize records (class ASSI 24/24-8 and ASSI 23/5) is a series of transportation order books of the Western Circuit (covering Devon, Cornwall, Dorset, Somerset, and Wiltshire), dating from 1629 to 1819. These list everyone sentenced to transportation, with the places and dates of trials. Among the Treasury papers (T1/437) there are a small number of certificates of transportation dated 1765, listing the names of transportees. These and other sources have been used to compile:

- Coldham Peter. *The Complete Book of Emigrants in Bondage, 1614–1775.* 9 vols in 3. Genealogical Publishing, 1998. Supplemented by *More Emigrants in Bondage 1614–1775.* Genealogical Publishing, 2002.

This is a revised version of:

- Coldham, P.W. *Bonded passengers to America.* 9 vols. in 3. Genealogical Publishing, 1983. v.1. History of transportation, 1615–1775. v.2. Middlesex, 1617–1775. v.3. London, 1656–1775. v.4. Home counties, 1655–1775. v.5. Western Circuit, 1664–1775. v.6. Oxford Circuit, 1663–1775. v.7. Norfolk Circuit, 1663–1775. v.8. Northern Circuit, 1665–1775. v.9. Midland Circuit, 1671–1775.

Transportation to North America ceased with the Declaration of American Independence in 1776. Temporarily, those sentenced to transportation were imprisoned in the hulks of warships which were no longer seaworthy. Eventually, a prison colony was established in Australia. The first fleet sailed in 1787. For brief biographies of those who sailed on the first two fleets, see:

- Gillen, Mollie. *The founders of Australia : a biographical dictionary of the first fleet.* Library of Australian History, 1989.
- Flynn, Michael. *The second fleet: Britain's grim convict armada of 1790.* Library of Australian History, 1993.

Lists of first and second fleeters are also available:

- Fidlon, P.G., and Ryan, R.J., eds. *The first fleeters: a comprehensive listing of convicts, marines, seamen, officers, wives, children and ships.* Australian Documents Library, 1981.
- Ryan, R.J., ed. *The second fleet convicts: a comprehensive listing of convicts who sailed in HMS Guardian, Lady Juliana, Neptune, Scarborough and Surprise.* Australian Documents Library, 1982.

Convict Transportation Registers in HO 11 list 123,000 convicts transported to Australia in various ships between 1787 and 1867, giving the dates of convictions, places of trial, terms of years, names of ships, places of arrival, and miscellaneous notes. The unindexed registers can be downloaded from TNA's digital microform page. They are indexed on the State Library of Queensland's Convict Transportation Registers Database **www.slq.qld.gov.au/resources/family-history/convicts** (scroll to the bottom of the page). For London and Middlesex transportees, see **www. digitalpanopticon.org/British_Transportation_Registers_1787-1867**

Convict indents are the official lists of convicts transported aboard particular ships, and are held by the State Records Authority of New South Wales. The earliest indents give names, trial dates, and sentences. Later records provide much more detail, such as ages, crimes, children, and much other useful information. A database is available at:

- New South Wales, Australia, Convict Indents, 1788–1842
  https://search.ancestry.co.uk/search/db.aspx?dbid=2024

The convict lists in HO 10 include details of sentences, employment, lists of pardons granted and other information concerning convicts and former convicts in Tasmania and New South Wales. They also include lists of convicts embarked for and arriving in New South Wales, various muster lists, and the 1828 census of settlers and convicts.[9] Unindexed volumes from this series may be downloaded from TNA's digital microform page. Many muster lists from this series, together with the 1828 census, are digitised at **www. ancestry.co.uk**.

During the journey to Australia, ships' surgeons compiled journals. Their content varies, but frequently includes detailed accounts of daily life aboard ships. Many convicts' names are recorded in these journals. Their health, their behaviour, and punishments administered, all sometimes attracted comment. For example, a list of convicts aboard the ship *Merchantman*, embarked at Bermuda for Western Australia in 1862, records that Edward Kelly had 'his wine stopped until further orders' for 'attempting to pass a counterfeit coin'.[10] Surgeons' journals are in ADM 101 and MT 32;

Bill Thompson, a Tasmanian convict, wearing leg irons and a uniform.

some in ADM 101 have been digitised in the National Archives microfilm project. See also:

- UK Surgeon Superintendents' Journals of Convict Ships, 1858–1867 **https://search.ancestry.co.uk/search/db.aspx?dbid=2320**

Convict entry books compiled in New South Wales, 1788–1868, now held by the Archives Authority of New South Wales, include a list of convicts arriving on transports, 1788–1800, an index to convict indents 1801–18, convict ships' musters on arrival (noting the persons to whom convicts were assigned), and other sources. The information in them may include convicts' trades or occupations, the places of conviction, sentences, and physical descriptions. The National Archives holds microfilm in CO 207.

Not everyone sentenced to transportation was actually transported. Some served out their entire sentences on convict hulks, or died there. Registers of convict hulks[11] 1802–1849 in HO 9 have been digitised for the National Archives digital microfilm webpage **www.nationalarchives. gov.uk/help-with-your-research/research-guides/free-online-records-digital-microfilm**. They are also available at **https://search.ancestry. co.uk/search/db.aspx?dbid=1989**. Further registers, 1825–35, are in ADM6/418-23, and, for 1849–60, PCOM 2/131-7. There are also quarterly lists of prisoners on convict hulks, 1828–61, in HO 8. This class also includes lists from other convict prisons up until 1876, together with

Ruins of the Penitentiary at Port Arthur, Tasmania.

a few for hulks at Bermuda.[12] These volumes record ages, convictions, sentences, health, and behaviour, and can be searched at **https://search.findmypast.co.uk/search-world-Records/prison-ship-hulk-registers**. Further quarterly lists for 1802–18 are in T 38/310-38.

Various convict records held by the Tasmanian Archive and Heritage Office have been digitised. See:

- Libraries Tasmania: Convict Life
  https://libraries.tas.gov.au/family-history/Pages/Convict-life.aspx
- Tasmania Convict Records 1800–1893
  www.findmypast.co.uk/articles/world-records/full-list-of-australia-and-new-zealand-records/institutions-and-organisations/tasmania-convict-records-1800-1893

For those convicted in London and Middlesex, see:

- My Ancestor was a Convict
  www.cityoflondon.gov.uk/things-to-do/london-metropolitan-archives/visitor-information/Documents/42-my-ancestor-was-a-convict.pdf

Transportees from Gloucestershire are listed in:

- Wyatt, Irene, ed. *Transportees from Gloucestershire to Australia 1783–1842*. Gloucestershire Record Series 1. Bristol & Gloucestershire Archaeological Society, 1988.

Lincolnshire's Convicts and Victims database can be searched from:

- Lincolnshire Convicts Transported
  www.lincolnshire.gov.uk/libraries-and-archives/lincolnshire-archives/archives-collections/lincolnshire-convicts-transported

A detailed guide to sources available in the UK, which is still useful despite the fact that it is too old to mention the internet, is provided by:

- Hawkings, David T. *Bound for Australia*. Phillimore, 1987.

Two online guides are also available:

- Convicts to Australia: a Guide to Researching your Convict Ancestors
  http://members.iinet.net.au/~perthdps/convicts/ships.html

- Convict Transportation
  www.nationalarchives.gov.uk/help-with-your-research/research-guides/criminal-transportation

For London see:

- Digital Panopticon: Tracing London Convicts in Britain & Australia, 1780–1925
  www.digitalpanopticon.org
  This site also includes brief lives of many convicts.

The workings of the transportation system are examined in detail and placed in their context by:

- Oldham, Wilfrid. *Britain's Convicts to the Colonies.* Library of Australian History, 1990. This covers both American and Australian transportation.
- Ekirch, A. Roger. *Bound for America: the Transportation of British Convicts to the Colonies 1718–1775.* Clarendon Press, 1987.
- Morgan, Gwenda, and Rushton, Peter. *Eighteenth-century Criminal Transportation: the Formation of the Criminal Atlantic.* Palgrave Macmillan, 2004.
- Coldham, Peter Wilson. *Emigrants in Chains: a social history of forced emigration to the Americas, 1607–1776.* Alan Sutton, 1992.
- Shaw, A.G.L. *Convicts and the Colonies: a study of penal transportation from Great Britain and Ireland to Australia and other parts of the British Empire.* Melbourne University Press, 1978.

Capital Punishment

Convicted felons who were not reprieved suffered capital punishment. For a full listing of executions, 1735–1964, together with details of many individual cases, and other useful information, visit:

- Capital Punishment UK
  www.capitalpunishmentuk.org

Chapter 9

DEBTORS AND BANKRUPTS

Introduction

Most of this book is focused on paupers and the labouring poor. Many debtors and bankrupts were not of this class. By definition, they were poor, but many were actually drawn from the middle classes, and even the gentry, who had become entangled in debt. Nevertheless, they were undoubtedly socially downwardly mobile, and there were some labourers among them, so it is appropriate to devote some attention to them here.

Until 1869, debtors could be imprisoned by their creditors. Crown debtors had been liable to imprisonment since 1159; private debtors since 1352. Debtors were subject to proceedings at common law, initiated by their creditors. The latter might summons them to appear in court. Debtors could be arrested and imprisoned until the court hearing. If, at trial, a debt was found to be good, the creditor could 'proceed in execution' by either having the sheriff seize and sell the debtor's goods (although landed property could not be seized), or by having the debtor imprisoned until the debt was paid. Imprisonment was often favoured by debtors, since the process of execution was fraught with difficulties. The process has been described as a 'system of legalized bullying', rather than 'a system of court supervised arbitration'.[1] Most creditors, however, only took action if they thought they could recover their debts. And some prisoners may have preferred to stay in prison: if they did, their goods could not be seized. From 1759, imprisoned debtors were legally entitled to claim a subsistence payment of 2s 4d per week from their creditors (although they frequently failed to obtain it).[2] They were sometimes eligible for help from charities, and might even be able to claim poor relief from overseers. In some gaols there were begging grates which allowed prisoners to solicit alms from passers-by.

A debtor at the begging grate in the Fleet Prison.

In the late seventeenth and eighteenth century, the recovery of small debts was made easier by the creation of courts of request, or conscience courts. These were local courts, each created by separate Acts of Parliament as the result of a petition from their borough. In the 1820s, they were hearing perhaps 200,000 cases per year.[3] In 1847, these were replaced by a new system of county courts, which, from 1869, also dealt with bankruptcy. These were extraordinarily popular with creditors, and an enormous number of cases were heard. Many defendants in these courts followed plebeian occupations, although they were likely to be married and older than criminals.

For most of the period covered by this book, debtors formed a substantial proportion of the prisoners incarcerated in county gaols, or in one of the London debtors' prisons, which included the Fleet (closed 1842), Faringdon (closed 1846), King's Bench, Southwark (closed 1880), Whitecross Street, Islington (closed 1870) and the Marshalsea, Southwark (closed 1842).[4] The Palace Court, which had its own prison, was used for the recovery of small debts in the Westminster area between 1630 and 1849.

Debtors could be incarcerated for years, although, from the 1780s, a limit was placed on the term served by small debtors.[5] With that exception, their release depended upon creditors, unless they were eligible to apply for bankruptcy. Bankruptcy was a process in which a court official took over the assets of the bankrupt and distributed them to creditors in proportion to what they owed. An Act of 1570 gave the Lord Chancellor the power to appoint commissioners, attached to the Court of Chancery, with powers over the person and property of a bankrupt. But only traders, that is, those who lived by buying and selling, could be bankrupts. In practice, by the eighteenth century most tradesmen were regarded as eligible for that status, and many others described themselves fictitiously as dealers or chapmen in their bankruptcy petitions. Non-traders could not be bankrupts; they were termed insolvents. An Act of 1705 gave the Lord Chancellor power to discharge bankrupts. However, only creditors could apply for discharge.

In 1772, the Society for the Relief and Discharge of Persons Imprisoned for Small Debts (frequently referred to as the Thatched House Society) was formed. Its funds enabled no fewer than 51,250 small debtors to gain their release, at an average cost of just under £3.[6] A variety of other charities performed similar functions; for example, sixty-four debtors were freed by a charity run by London's Ironmongers Company between 1752 and 1761.[7] In Gloucestershire, the Prison Charity Committee minutes record the names of many debtors, and provide substantial information on individual traits used to distinguish between the deserving and the undeserving.[8]

An Act of 1813 created the Insolvent Debtors Court, which could hear petitions from prisoners seeking release; they had to swear that they were worth no more than £20 – but even then creditors had to agree to their release. From 1825, debtors were able to commence proceedings for their own bankruptcy, in agreement with creditors. Their declarations of insolvency were advertised in the London Gazette, after which the Lord Chancellor could issue a commission in bankruptcy.

From 1832, the newly established Court of Bankruptcy took over the bankruptcy jurisdiction formerly exercised by the Court of Chancery. In 1842, district bankruptcy courts were also established. These were abolished in 1869, when their jurisdiction was mostly transferred to the County Courts. The London Court of Bankruptcy was to hear local cases, and also appeals from the County Courts. It was incorporated into the Supreme Court of Judicature, as the High Court of Justice in Bankruptcy, in 1883. The 1883 Act also established an official receiver of debtors' estates within the Board of Trade.

The distinction between bankrupts and insolvent debtors was ended by the Bankruptcy Act, 1861, which transferred jurisdiction of the

Insolvent Debtors Court to the Bankruptcy Court. Imprisonment for debt was ended by the Debtors' Act 1869, except for debtors committed by County Courts for contempt of court. That Act was accompanied by the Bankruptcy Act 1869, which extended the right to petition for bankruptcy to everyone, not just traders.[9] County court imprisonment was finally abolished in 1970.[10] For a detailed discussion of the various acts relating to debt and bankruptcy, visit **http://discovery.nationalarchives.gov.uk/ details/r/C23**.

Sources: Insolvent Debtors

Proceedings against debtors took place in the central civil courts, or in borough and other local courts of record such as those mentioned above. The role of the former was, of course, much wider than mere debt recovery, and most of their records are beyond the scope of this book. For a useful introduction, see:

- Moore, Susan. *Tracing your Ancestors through the Equity Courts: a guide for Family and Local Historians.* Pen & Sword, 2017.

Debtors imprisoned between 1628 and 1862 in the Fleet Prison, King's Bench (or Queen's Prison), and the Marshalsea may be identified in The National Archives classes PRIS 1–12. These include commitment books naming prisoners committed, the commitment number (which may be useful in tracing prisoners' records), and sometimes with additional information. Commitment files trace the process of commitment; warrants trace their discharge. Marshalsea Commitment books 1811–1842 (from PRIS 11–12) have been digitised by Ancestry; see **https:// search.ancestry.co.uk/search/db.aspx?dbid=9159**. A variety of records relating to the Fleet Prison and the Marshalsea 1734–1862 are digitised at **https://search.ancestry.co.uk/search/db.aspx?dbid=9158**. For records of the Palace Court, see PALA 1–9. Returns of insolvents in some other London prisons, 1828–1883 are in B 2.

The National Archives also hold various lists of debtors imprisoned in the provinces. For example, 1,200 debtors in Lincoln gaol 1810–1822 are listed by PCOM2/309. Similar lists for debtors in Shrewsbury gaol, 1855–61 are in PCOM 2/396, and for Lancaster, 1792–7, in PCOM 2/440. Debtors' applications for release from prison in the Palatinate of Cheshire, 1760–1830, are in CHES 10.

Thatched House Society archives are held by London Metropolitan Archives. Its minutes, which run from 1772–1872, name the debtors helped by the society. Some of its petitions for the discharge of prisoners are in The National Archives, PRIS 10/238.

Petitions to the Insolvent Debtors' Court are in B 6/45–71. Some indexes to these classes are in B 7 and B 8. Petitions for release from imprisoned debtors were printed in the *London Gazette*. This court delegated some of its powers to Quarter Sessions, and from 1824 was empowered to go on circuit itself. Gloucestershire Archives holds minutes of proceedings in cases of insolvent debtors, 1824–1847;[11] similar records may be available in other local record offices. Debtors frequently petitioned Parliament for relief; their petitions are held by the Parliamentary Archives. For example, debtors in Warwick Gaol petitioned Parliament in 1795.[12]

A few records of local courts of requests, and of the nineteenth-century county courts, are available in local record offices, although survival of those from courts of requests is poor.[13] A central registry of county court judgements was established in 1852; its registers are in The National Archives, LCO 28.[14] For 1870–84, registers of cases heard in county courts are in BT 40/34–52. Registers of cases heard in the London Bankruptcy Court, 1870–86, are in BT 40/25–33. Between 1884 and 1923, registers of everyone served with petitions for bankruptcy are in BT 293. Miscellaneous papers of the official receiver, dealing with bankruptcy cases in the High Court, 1891–1994, are in BT 226.

Useful information concerning imprisoned debtors may also be found among Quarter Sessions and other courts' records in local record offices. For example, Wiltshire and Swindon History Centre has lists of debtors imprisoned in the county gaol at Fisherton Anger, 1724–81, together with petitions for discharge, and schedules of prisoners' real and personal estates.[15] Devon Heritage Centre has many petitions for release from prison by insolvent debtors.

Sources: Bankrupts

The earliest records of bankruptcy are to be found among pleadings in the Court of Chancery, which exercised jurisdiction until 1832. Use the advanced search facility at **http://discovery.nationalarchives.gov.uk** to search for bankrupts by name and keyword 'bankrupt' or 'creditor' in department code 'C'. The Close rolls (C 54) contain conveyances of bankrupts' estates. Miscellaneous exhibits in bankruptcy cases for the sixteenth century and later can be found in C 217.

The *London Gazette* **www.thegazette.co.uk** is the first port of call for tracing bankruptcy proceedings after 1727. Official notices of bankruptcy proceedings, and of the names of petitioners to the Insolvent Debtors Court (after 1813) were published here in order to keep creditors informed. This information was also published in *The Times* and other newspapers. Many newspapers have been digitised by the British Newspaper Archive **www.britishnewspaperarchive.co.uk**, which is worth searching for the names of bankrupts and insolvents. After 1862, official notices concerning proceedings in county courts (see below) were regularly placed in local newspapers.

Two summary listings of bankrupts have been published:

- *An Alphabetical List of all the Bankrupts from the First of January 1774 to the Thirtieth of June 1786... .* J. Jarvis, 1786. Reproduced on fiche, Society of Genealogists.
- Elwick, George. *The Bankrupt Directory, being a complete register of all the bankrupts, with their residences, trades, and dates when they appeared in the London Gazette, from December 1820 to April 1843.* Simpkin, Marshall & Co., 1843. Online at **archive.org**

Finding an entry in the *London Gazette* will enable you to search the bankruptcy records in The National Archives and elsewhere. The records of the Bankruptcy Commissioners and their successors, 1733–1925, are held in the B classes, although much has been lost. There are a variety of registers, which may sometimes add a small amount of information to the *London Gazette* entry. Not many case files survive, but those which do are likely to provide more detailed information. Docket books recording the issue of commissions, together with registers of commissions of bankruptcy, 1710–1849, are in B 4. Commissions themselves, together with a variety of other documents, are enrolled in B 5. If an entry in the B 4 registers is underlined, the relevant case file should survive in B 3. These include examinations of bankrupts, lists of creditors, etc., from the period 1753–1854. Other case files, from 1832 onwards, are in B 9. Declarations of insolvency and inability to pay, 1825–1925 are in classes B 6/74–8, B 6/176–177 and B 6/220–222. After 1854, these records only cover London. The information they provide include the date of the declaration, the name, address and occupation of the debtor, and the name of the debtor's solicitor.

Further Reading
A useful guide to sources is provided by:

- Bankrupts and insolvent debtors
  www.nationalarchives.gov.uk/help-with-your-research/research-guides/bankrupts-insolvent-debtors

See also Chapter 3 of:

- Cale, Michelle. *Law and Society: an introduction to Sources for Criminal and Legal History from 1800.* PRO Publications, 1996.

For London, see:

- London Metropolitan Archives Information Leaflet 66: Imprisoned debtors
  www.cityoflondon.gov.uk/things-to-do/london-metropolitan-archives/visitor-information/Documents/66-imprisoned-debtors.pdf

For a popular history of debt, see:

- Barty-King, Hugh. *The worst poverty: a history of debt and debtors.* Alan Sutton, 1991.

A study of imprisonment for debt, drawing on a wide range of sources, is included in:

- Finn, Margot C. *The Character of Credit: Personal Debt in English Culture, 1740–1914.* Cambridge University Press, 2003.

A chapter on 'the debtor's world' is included in:

- White, Jerry. *Mansions of Misery: a Biography of the Marshalsea Debtors' Prison.* Bodley Head, 2016.

For a study of a debtors' prison, which includes a useful outline of debt procedure, see:

- Innes, Joanna. 'The King's Bench Prison in the later eighteenth century: law, authority and order in a London Debtors' Prison', in Brewer, John, and Styles, John, eds. *An Ungovernable People? The English and their Law in the seventeenth and eighteenth centuries.* Hutchinson, 1980, p.250–61.

Chapter 10

MISCELLANEOUS SOURCES

Adoption

Before 1927, it was not possible to legally adopt a child. Adopters therefore had no legal rights over adoptees, and parents could demand that a child be returned to them at any time. However, the great majority of adopted children were illegitimate and poor. For these the common law principle of *filius nullius* applied. This principle stated that bastards did not belong to anyone. Even birth mothers had no rights over them, so adopters had some protection.

In the late nineteenth and early twentieth century, a number of institutions acted as adoption agencies. The Salvation Army was one of these. Its records are rather fragmentary, but do include some copies of forms used since 1902 to record details of children, together with requests for adoption, and legal adoption agreements.[1] Some other adoption agencies kept full files including photographs, correspondence, and details of next of kin – which may be subject to stringent access conditions.

The Adoption Act 1927 provided a legally enforceable method for transferring parental rights. Initially, it was thought best that adoptees should have no contact with their birth families, so they were registered in the Adopted Children's Registers, and adoptees were issued with adoption certificates rather than birth certificates. However, contact has been possible since 1975, and birth certificates can be made available. For those adopted before 1975, it is necessary to attend a counselling session first. For details, see:

- Adoption Records
  www.gov.uk/adoption-records

This page includes the Adoption Contact Register, which may assist you in making contact with birth relatives. For a detailed guide to adoption records, see:

- Bali, Karen. *Researching Adoption: an essential guide to tracing birth relatives and ancestors.* Family History Partnership, 2015.

The history of adoption is outlined, and advice on sources is given, in:

- Rossini, Gill. *A History of Adoption in England and Wales, 1850 to 1961.* Pen & Sword, 2014.

Bridewell

Even before the introduction of the Elizabethan poor law in 1597, there were various experiments with workhouses. Bridewell was a former royal residence that was transformed into an institution for the poor in 1553. Its role was to be a cross between a workhouse, a reformatory, and a prison. It housed vagrants and the disorderly poor, who were supposed to benefit from the harsh regime of daily labour and strict discipline. Bridewell archives are now held by London Metropolitan Archives.

Prisoners could be committed to Bridewell by constables and magistrates; they could also be placed there by masters, and even by parents. From 1785, only Justices of the Peace could make commitments. Many were committed for vice, vagrancy, and property crimes. The names of prisoners can be found in Warrants of Commitment and Discharge (PM), and in the Minutes of the Court of Governors (MG).

Bridewell also served as an orphanage. The boys were taught reading and writing, and apprenticed to an arts master within the institution; they learnt trades such as weaving, shoemaking and glovemaking. They were not, however, pauper apprentices, and could expect to become freemen of the City of London, and to receive £10 from a charity, on successful completion of their apprenticeships. They are listed in registers of apprentices, and mentioned in various minute books.

The London Bridewell served as a model for the subsequent development of Houses of Correction (see above, p.31). References to Bridewell frequently relate to provincial Bridewells, and not to the original London institution.

Some Bridewell records have been digitised at:

- London Lives 1690 to 1800: Miscellaneous Parish and Bridewell Papers (PM)
  www.londonlives.org/static/PM.jsp#Bridewell

See also:

- Bridewell House of Correction Prisoners 1740–1795
  www.digitalpanopticon.org/Bridewell_House_of_Correction_Prisoners_1740-1795

For a general history, see:

- Hinkle, William G. *A History of Bridewell Prison, 1553–1700*. Edwin Mellen Press, 2006.

The Census

A number of introductions to the census are available,[2] and this is not the place to provide a detailed guide. However, workhouses, prisons, and other institutions were given special treatment. Census schedules were devised which gave only the name and address of the institution, not the home addresses of inmates. The master or the governor usually completed census schedules. Preliminary tables record the numbers of officers, members of officers' families, and inmates. In 1851, there was a column for 'position in the institution'; in subsequent censuses, this was for 'relation to the head of family or position in the institution'. In practice, unless more than one member of a family was present, relationships were not given. Enumerators frequently tried to preserve the anonymity of inmates by giving initials only. Workhouse masters frequently did not have accurate details of inmates' ages, places of birth, and occupations, and sometimes either made informed guesses, or wrote 'NK' – not known. The usefulness of the census for tracing the institutionalised is therefore more limited than usual.

For prisons, a number of indexes to census records are available at:

- Blacksheep Ancestors United Kingdom
  www.blacksheepancestors.com/uk

Civil Registration

The civil registers are outside of the scope of this book. However, it is worth pointing out that, from 1834, birth and death registers identified workhouse inmates by writing W in the margin of the entry. In 1904, this practice ceased in the birth register; registrars were instructed to conceal workhouse births by merely giving a street address, or perhaps even a fictitious address, rather than the name of the institution.[3] For example, births registered at St. Pancras Workhouse are recorded as having taken place at 4, Kings Road, St Pancras. The same change in practice was implemented for death entries in 1919. If a place of birth or death given on a civil registration certificate is somewhere other than the family's usual place of residence, it is worth checking to see whether it was a workhouse, perhaps by checking a trade directory (see below, pp.171–2).

Cottages

An Act of 1589 prohibited the erection of cottages by the poor unless they had four acres of land attached. The purpose was to reduce rural poverty by preventing over-population in parishes where there were insufficient opportunities for employment. Quarter Sessions, however, could permit building to take place. There are many petitions and habitation orders relating to the provision of new cottages among Quarter Sessions rolls, with details sometimes entered in order books. For example, in 1662, William Grant petitioned the Justices for permission to erect a new cottage at Imber (Wiltshire), as he had been 'warned to depart his house', and he and his family of five small children were 'likely in short tyme to bee harbourlesses and thereby to fall into unexpressible misery'. He had obtained the support of 'the greatest parte of ye inhabitons' for his petition.[4] Such petitions record the presence of the petitioners in place and time, may give details of their families, and sometimes also mention the names of other parishioners.

Diaries

Diaries of those associated with the poor in any way may provide a great deal of information. The master of Barnet Workhouse left one such diary. It identifies numerous paupers, and has been published with brief extracts from the Workhouse Admission and Discharge Register, and from a register of paupers for whom places in service had been found. See:

• Gear, Gillian, ed. *The Diary of Benjamin Woodcock, Master of the Barnet Union Workhouse, 1836–1838.* Hertfordshire Record Publications, 24. 2008.

Emigration

We have already seen that many poor children were sent to Canada, Australia, and other colonies by charities, that many felons were transported to North America and Australia, and that some paupers received assistance to emigrate from the Poor Law authorities. Many other poor emigrants were funded by the Colonial Land and Emigration

Commissioners (CLEC), established in 1833 to provide a programme of free or assisted emigration to colonies such as Canada, Australia and New Zealand. It was renamed the Emigration Commission in 1855. The Commissioners' original remit specifically excluded recipients of poor relief, although after 1848 paupers were allowed to benefit. By 1869, about 300,000 emigrants had been assisted. Registers of emigrants to Canada, 1850–68, are in CO 327–8. Correspondence from the Commissioners and related bodies, 1817–96, in CO 384–6, mentions many names.

For more recent emigrants, it may be useful to consult the outgoing passenger lists of the Board of Trade, 1890–1960. These are in BT 27, and have been digitised at:

- Passenger Lists Leaving UK 1890–1960
  https://search.findmypast.co.uk/search-world-Records/passenger-lists-leaving-uk-1890-1960

For a detailed guide to migration records, see:

- Kershaw, Roger. *Migration Records: a Guide for Family Historians*. The National Archives, 2009.

See also the National Archives webpage on:

- Emigration and Emigrants
  www.nationalarchives.gov.uk/help-with-your-research/research-guides/emigration

A full listing of emigrants to North America prior to 1776 is provided by:

- Coldham, P.W. *The complete book of emigrants, 1607–1660: a comprehensive listing compiled from English public records of those who took ship to the Americas for political, religious, and economic reasons; of those who were deported for vagrancy, roguery, or non-conformity; and of those who were sold to labour in the new colonies.* Baltimore: Genealogical Publishing, 1987. Further volumes cover 1661–99 (1990), 1700–1750 (1992), and 1751–1776 (1993).

Various databases and other information relating to immigrants in Ontario, including indexes to the Toronto Emigrant Office Assisted Immigration Registers, 1865–83, may be located at:

- Archives of Ontario: Finding Immigration Records
  **www.archives.gov.on.ca/en/access/documents/research_guide_228_
  immigration_citizenship.pdf**

Friendly Societies

Friendly societies were mutual aid societies which insured their members (mostly poor) against illness, unemployment, death, and/or other eventualities. Most were local, but a few were county-wide or even national. Many were founded in the late eighteenth century; they flourished in the nineteenth century, but membership rapidly declined after the National Insurance Act 1911 inaugurated the Welfare State. Rose's Act, 1793, and subsequent legislation gave them statutory protection from embezzlement, misappropriation and theft. Early societies were listed in a *Return relating to Friendly Societies* published in Parliamentary Paper 1837/51. In 1846, the Registrar of Friendly Societies was established. His reports were published in the Parliamentary papers series (see above, pp.5–6). On appointment, the Registrar collected rules made under the 1793 Act; his collection is now among the FS classes. Some files in these classes also include correspondence and member lists of dissolved societies. Rules may sometimes also be found among Quarter Sessions records in local record offices.

The records of the societies themselves frequently do not survive. That, however, is not invariable, and many can be identified via **http:// discovery.nationalarchives.gov.uk**. An interesting example is provided by the membership and subscription book of a Colyton (Devon) burial book, which lists its members in the order in which they were to walk in procession, and includes occasional notes of funerals, 1809–38.[5] Another example is provided by the Birmingham Roman Catholic Friendly Society, established as a 'sick club' in 1795, with thirty-seven subscribers. It provided financial assistance to sick members, to defray funeral costs, and to make provision for widows and dependants. Being a Catholic organisation, it also offered masses for both living and deceased members. At the end of the nineteenth century, it had around 200 members. The Society's archives up to 1945 are held by the Archdiocese of Birmingham Archives **http://birminghamarchdiocesanarchives.org.uk/collections. asp**. They primarily consist of minutes and registers of members. The latter record names, ages, residences, trades, proposers, dates of election, and premiums paid.

The Oddfellows **www.oddfellows.co.uk/OnlineArchives**, and the Foresters **www.aoforestersheritage.com** are two of the largest friendly societies. Both preserve membership registers, which may reveal useful information about your ancestors. Annual directories of the Oddfellows, together with the *Oddfellows Magazine*, contain much information on members. Many issues can be found on the digitised book sites mentioned above (pp.3–4); copies can sometimes also be found in libraries.

Further Reading
The history of friendly societies is outlined in:

• Cordery, Simon. *British Friendly Societies, 1750–1914*. Palgrave Macmillan, 2003.

See also:

• Gosden, P.H.J.H. *The Friendly Societies in England, 1815–1875*. Manchester University Press, 1961.
• Fuller, Margaret D. *West Country Friendly Societies*. University of Reading, 1964.

For a brief guide to records, see:

• Weinbren, David. *Tracing your Freemason, Friendly Society and Trade Union Ancestors: A Guide for Family Historians*. Pen & Sword, 2019.

Records from a variety of sources, and from 755 societies, have been edited in:

• Morley, Shaun, ed. *Oxfordshire Friendly Societies 1750–1918*. Oxfordshire Record Series, 68. 2011.

Hearth Tax
The poor frequently did not pay tax. Some tax records, however, identify those who were exempt. Hearth tax exemption certificates are particularly useful in this regard. From Michaelmas 1663, exempt householders had to be included on returns as well as those who were chargeable. Exemption certificates survive randomly in the 1660s and 1670s, many of them printed. These were prepared by local ministers, signed by churchwardens, overseers, and Justices of the Peace. Names from them were copied into the returns as 'persons discharged' or 'not chargeable'. Exemption could only be claimed by those who had only one or two hearths. Some poor drifted in and out of chargeability, being exempt in one year, but charged the next.

Documentation occasionally survives in local record offices, but an extensive collection of tax documents, including many relating to the hearth tax, is in E179. These are fully listed by:

- E179 Database
  www.nationalarchives.gov.uk/e179

Many exemption certificates, especially for East Anglia, have been published by the British Record Society. See, for example:

- Seaman, Peter, ed. *Norfolk Hearth Tax Exemption Certificates 1670–1674: Norwich, Great Yarmouth, King's Lynn and Thetford.* Hearth Tax series 3. British Record Society. 2001. Also published by Norfolk Record Society as its vol.65.

For more information on the hearth tax, visit:

- Hearth Tax Online
  https://hearthtax.wordpress.com

Lunatic Asylums

The earliest English asylum for the mentally ill (who were usually termed lunatics) was London's Bethlem (or Bedlam) Hospital. It was founded in 1247 to house a religious order caring for the sick, and gradually came to specialise in caring for the mentally ill, but was

Bethlem Hospital in St. George's Fields, by Thomas Shepherd.

Sheriff Hill Lunatic Asylum, Gateshead.

dissolved in 1533 with other monasteries. In 1547 it was refounded by the Corporation of London. Its archives are held by Bethlem Museum of the Mind **http://museumofthemind.org.uk/collections/archives**. They include admission registers and casebooks 1683–1932, available on Find My Past **www.findmypast.co.uk**. Criminal lunatic asylum registers from Bethlem, 1820–1843, are in HO 20, and are digitised at **https://search. ancestry.co.uk/search/db.aspx?dbid=9163**. From the 1570s, it was governed jointly with Bridewell (see pp.157–8); the minutes of the Court of Governors 1689–1800 can be read online at **www.londonlives.org/ static/Bridewell.jsp**.

For centuries, Bethlem was the only specialist public institution for lunatics. Until the nineteenth century, most poor lunatics were relieved by overseers under the supervision of Quarter Sessions. Many were confined in workhouses or Houses of Correction. There were also a few private asylums, which, from 1774, had to be licensed by Quarter Sessions. Paupers were occasionally sent to them. A register of private asylums, 1798–1812, listing patients admitted, is in MH 51/735.

It was not until the nineteenth century that specialist public asylums were founded. In 1808, Quarter Sessions were authorised to build county lunatic asylums. However, not all counties did so until they became compulsory in 1845. Even then, many lunatics remained in

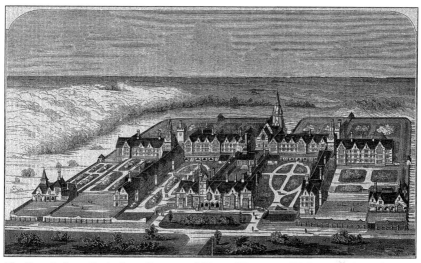

The County Lunatic Asylum, Brentwood, Essex. (Courtesy Wellcome Library)

union workhouses. Asylums were more expensive to run, and in any case there were not enough of them. In 1858, there were 31,510 pauper insane in England and Wales.[6] Three years later, a survey found that 35% of those who had been resident in workhouses for more than five years suffered from 'mental disease'.[7]

Admittance to the county asylum was authorised by Justices of the Peace, usually by application of a parish overseer, or, after 1834, a union relieving officer. After 1845, union medical officers also had to sign applications. Admission documents, likely to be in local record offices, are particularly useful, since they contain much information provided by relieving officers and medical officers. Some asylum records have been digitised; for example, Find My Past **www.findmypast.co.uk** holds databases of Prestwich Asylum admission registers, 1851–1901, South Yorkshire Asylum admission registers 1872–1910, and Bexley Asylum Minute Books, 1901–1939.

FIRST REPORT

OF THE

SOMERSET COUNTY ASYLUM,

FOR INSANE PAUPERS,

FROM THE 1st MARCH,

WHEN IT WAS OPENED FOR PATIENTS,

TO THE END OF THE YEAR

1848.

WELLS:

PRINTED BY SAMUEL BACKHOUSE, HIGH STREET.

1849.

The 1st report from Somerset County Asylum

After 1845, copies of admission registers from both public and private asylums had to be sent to the Lunacy Commission and its successors.

The City Lunatic Asylum, near Dartford. Courtesy Wellcome Library.

These record the names of patients, institutions, dates of admission, and dates of discharge or death. Registers prior to 1960 are now in class MH 94. Some – but not all – of these have been digitised at:

- UK, Lunacy Patients Admission Registers, 1846–1912
  https://search.ancestry.co.uk/search/db.aspx?dbid=9051

Pauper lunatics sent to county asylums remained the responsibility of poor law unions. The archives of the latter (see Chapter 5) frequently include references to them. For example, the Alderbury Union (Wiltshire) has a listing of 'lunatic paupers in the Asylums chargeable to the Union' for six months prior to Lady Day 1896.[8]

Under Acts of 1815 and 1828, parish overseers were required to make returns of pauper lunatics to Clerks of the Peace. After 1842, similar returns were made by Union clerks to the Poor Law Commissioners. The latter are now among poor law correspondence in class MH 12 (see above, pp.102–103). Various lists of lunatics in asylums in the mid-nineteenth century are in MH51/737-762. A very few patient records are in MH 85 and MH 86, and MH51/27–77.

Registers of Pauper Lunatics are likely to record names, dates of admission, the name of the person ordering admission, a description of the 'Lunacy, or Nature of Disease', details of examination on admission, and the medical officer's certificate of the reason for the lunacy. Early lists of pauper lunatics can also be found in class MH 12.

For criminal lunatics, there are sworn lists of convicts from 1862 until 1876 in HO 8/149–207, which can be searched at **www.findmypast.co.uk**.

Warrants for the removal of criminal lunatics from prisons to asylums, 1882–1921, are in HO 145, partially digitised at **https://search.ancestry. co.uk/search/db.aspx?dbid=9162**. Some papers relating to individual criminal lunatics are in HO 144. In 1858, returns of insane prisoners in prisons and Houses of Correction were made to the Lunacy Commission. These are in class MH 51/90–207.

Both county and private asylums maintained a wide variety of other records. Many can be located by consulting:

- Hospital Records Database
  www.nationalarchives.gov.uk/hospitalrecords

The Wellcome Library and other institutions are currently digitising over 800,000 pages of archival material from psychiatric institutions and mental health organisations in the UK. This will include registers and other patient records. For details of participating institutions and their collections, see:

- Wellcome Library Mental Healthcare
  https://wellcomelibrary.org/collections/digital-collections/mental-healthcare

Further Reading
For a detailed guide to sources for lunatics, see:

- Chater, Kathy. *My Ancestor was a Lunatic*. Society of Genealogists Enterprises, 2015.

See also:

- Lunatic asylums, psychiatric hospitals and mental health
  www.nationalarchives.gov.uk/help-with-your-research/research-guides/mental-health

Interesting introductions to the history of mental illness are provided by:

- Porter, Roy. *Madmen: A Social History of Madhouses, Mad-Doctors, & Lunatics*. Tempus, 2004.
- Scull, Andrew. *The Most Solitary of Afflictions: Madness and Society in Britain, 1700–1900*. Yale University Press, 1993.

Maimed Soldiers

Sixteenth- and seventeenth-century wars resulted in many wounded soldiers, who needed support. Together with their wives, widows, and children, they were frequently forced to resort to the poor law. Better provision for their support began in 1593, when Parliament authorised Quarter Sessions to grant pensions to maimed soldiers. Pensioners can frequently be identified through accounts, through their petitions, and through letters from their commanding officers supporting their petitions. Such documents are likely to be found among sessions rolls, although they may also be found in separate files among Quarter Sessions records. Civil War soldiers, of course, only received pensions when the side they had fought for were in power.

Letters from commanding officers are frequently found supporting applications for pensions. For example, in 1647 Sir William Waller wrote 'the bearer hereof Wm Dollery having binn employed under me in the service of the King and Parlmt: I doe hereby certify that he served as sarieant of a Company of Dragoons , & that duringe his service hee recd a wound on his right hand by wch hee hath lost the use of his hand'. He was given a pension of 13s 4d per annum.[9]

Petitions from other sources may also provide information on soldiers. In 1652, the overseers of Mere (Wiltshire) had received several sums of 40s towards the relief of Andrew Smyth from the treasurer of maimed soldiers, but complained to Quarter Sessions that 'be meanes of his desease wee are in noe way able to relieve him according to his necessity by reason of soe many poore within our said parish'. The bench agreed to a further payment of 40s 'for this time onely'.[10] It is not clear why Smyth was thought not to be eligible for a direct pension from the Treasurer, but was eligible for indirect support. But it seems possible that he had not actually been injured while fighting for Parliament, but had contracted 'desease'.

For the maimed soldiers of the Civil War, see:

• Gruber von Arni, Eric. *Justice to the maimed soldier: nursing, medical care and welfare for sick and wounded soldiers and their families during the English civil wars and interregnum, 1642–1660.* Ashgate, 2001.

Militia Lists

The Militia Act 1757 created militia regiments in every English and Welsh county, which were recruited by parish constables. The recruitment process required constables to prepare two lists of men aged eighteen to fifty (forty-five from 1762). Militia muster rolls listed all male parishioners. These were used in order to hold ballots to choose those who had to serve. Militia enrolment lists record the names of those actually chosen to serve. Those chosen could name substitutes to serve in their stead; these too were listed. Substitutes were frequently chosen from paupers and the poor. Muster books listing those who actually served can be found in The National Archives, class WO 13. These are transcribed and indexed for 1781–2 at **www.thegenealogist.co.uk**. It may be useful to check names found in these sources against the poor law records described in chapters 4 and 5.

Muster rolls and enrolment lists are generally found in county record offices, and sometimes in military museums. Their survival is patchy. A few are digitised at **www.ancestry.co.uk**. For a full directory of available lists, consult:

- Gibson, Jeremy, and Medlycott, Mervyn. *Militia lists and musters 1757–1876: a directory of holdings in the British Isles*. 5th ed. Family History Partnership, 2013.

For details of other militia records, see:

- Spencer, William. *Records of the Militia and Volunteer Forces 1757–1945*. Rev. ed. Readers Guide 3. Public Record Office, 1997.

Newspapers

Nineteenth- and twentieth-century newspapers frequently mention the poor. They thrived on lurid reports of criminal trials, they were paid to advertise information about pauper apprentices who had absconded, and they sometimes reported and commented extensively on poor law matters. It is quite likely that, at some stage in their lives, your poor ancestors were mentioned in a newspaper.

Until recently, newspapers were difficult to search. However, the advent of digitisation means that both local and national newspapers can now easily be searched. Numerous newspapers, both local and national, have been digitised for:

- British Newspaper Archive
  www.britishnewspaperarchive.co.uk.

A few newspapers are searchable on stand-alone sites. The most important of these is probably *The Times*. See:

- *The Times* Digital Archive, 1785–2013
  www.gale.com/intl/c/the-times-digital-archive

Both of these are subscription sites, which can sometimes be accessed free through local public library websites. See also **www.thetimes.co.uk/ subscribe/benefits/archives**.

It may also be worth checking periodical publications such as the *Annual Register*, the *Gentleman's Magazine*, the *Illustrated London News*, and *Household Words*, all of which regularly reported major trials. They have been digitised on various websites; for a web directory of these and other digitised journals, visit:

- The Online Books Page: Serials
  http://onlinebooks.library.upenn.edu/serials.html

Parish Registers

Parish registers of vital events are outside of the scope of this book.[11] It is, however, worth noting that they record (or possibly fail to record) the baptisms and burials of the poor. Although they are not generally identified as such in parish register entries, paupers were affected by two attempts to impose duties on entries. Both of these attempts had a deleterious effect on the keeping of registers, since the poor ceased to bring babies for baptism. Taxes were imposed between 1695 and 1705, and between 1783 and 1794. In the latter period, paupers were exempt, and entries were frequently annotated with the letter 'P' (for pauper) or 'EP' (exempt pauper). Children baptised immediately after the repeal of these Acts may have been older than the norm; their parents may have been unwilling to have them baptised if that meant paying tax.

Pawnbrokers

Pawnbrokers provided one means by which the poor could survive from day to day. Admittedly, not all of their customers were poor, and it is also true that pawnbrokers were wary of paupers and the completely destitute, who might be unable to redeem their goods. But there were many with regular or semi-regular wages – the 'industrious poor' – who needed cash prior to payday. They could borrow by pawning such goods as they owned until such time as they found sufficient money to redeem them. Typically, among the industrial working classes, a family might regularly pawn their Sunday best on Monday and redeem it on Saturday when the breadwinner had been paid. Half of all the pledges received by a York pawnbroker in September 1777 were redeemed within a month.[12] It was a frequent practice to buy valuable goods when cash was available so that they could be used as pawns when needed. This was a form of insurance against the inevitable future financial difficulties.[13]

In the nineteenth century pawnbrokers were mostly found in northern industrial centres, especially in Lancashire, although there were some in cities such as Plymouth and Bristol.[14] They were rare in rural areas.

Pawnbrokers' pledge books or registers, which were originally mandated by an Act of 1757, can occasionally be found in local record offices. These registers were required to detail the goods pledged, the money lent, the date, and the name and address of the pledger. If the goods belonged to someone else, then their name and address was also required. Registers are also likely to record the date of redemption. One York register records no fewer than 10,917 pledges made by perhaps 2,200 individuals between July 1777 and December 1778.[15]

For an interesting study of pawnbroking, see:

- Tebbutt, Melanie. *Making ends meet: pawnbroking and working-class credit*. Methuen, 1984.

See also:

- Hudson, Kenneth. *Pawnbroking: an Aspect of British History*. Bodley Head, 1982.

For a study of a York pawnbroker's register, see:

- 'Pawnbroking and the use of Credit', in Tomkins, Alannah. *The Experience of urban poverty, 1723–82: Parish, Charity, and Credit*. Manchester University Press, 2006, p.204–34.[16]

Trade Directories

Numerous trade directories were published in the nineteenth and twentieth century. These generally listed the middle and upper classes, rather than the poor. However, they did list institutions such as workhouses and orphanages that catered for the poor. If you need to identify such institutions, it may be useful to consult directories. Many are digitised online at:

- Historical Directories
  www2.le.ac.uk/library/find/specialcollections/specialcollections/historical-directories

Many other directories are held in local studies libraries and record offices. For full lists, with locations, see:

- Norton, Jane E. *Guide to the national and provincial directories of England and Wales, excluding London, published before 1856.* Royal Historical Society guides and handbooks 5. 1950.
- Shaw, Gareth, and Tipper, Alison. *British directories: a bibliography and guide to directories published in England and Wales (1850–1950) and Scotland (1773–1950).* 2nd ed. Mansell Publishing, 1997.

NOTES

Chapter 2: The History of the Poor

1. Hitchcock, Tim, & Shoemaker, Robert. *London Lives: Poverty, Crime and the Making of a Modern City. 1690–1800.* Cambridge University Press, 2015, p.5.
2. Beier, A.L. *The Problem of the Poor in Tudor and Early Stuart England.* Routledge Falmer, 1983, p.7.
3. Slack, Paul. *The English Poor Law, 1531–1782.* Cambridge University Press, 1995, p.4.
4. Quaife, G.R. *Wanton Wenches and Wayward Wives: peasants and illicit sex in early seventeenth century England.* Croom Helm, 1979, p.24, citing Walter, John, & Wrightson, Keith. 'Dearth and the Social Order in Early Modern England', *Past & Present,* 71, 1976, p.22–44.
5. Beier, A.L. *Masterless men: the Vagrancy problem in England 1560–1640.* Methuen, 1985, p.23.
6. Beier, *Masterless men,* op cit, p.31.
7. For the sources of these statistics, see Beier, *Masterless men,* op cit, pp.16–17. See also King, Steven, Nutt, Thomas, & Tomkins, Alannah, eds. *Narratives of the Poor in Eighteenth-Century Britain. Vol. 1: Voices of the Poor: Poor Law Depositions and Letters.* Pickering & Chatto, 2006, p.x.
8. Wiltshire & Swindon History Centre A1/110/H1627/111.
9. Sharp, Buchanan. *In contempt of all authority: rural artisans and riot in the West of England, 1586–1660.* University of California Press, 1980, p.258.
10. Beier, *Problem of the Poor,* op cit, p.9.
11. Hitchcock, Tim, King, Peter, & Sharpe, Pamela, eds. *Chronicling Poverty: the Voices and Strategies of the English Poor, 1640–1840.* Macmillan Press, 1997, p.10.
12. Snell, K.D.M. *Annals of the Labouring Poor: Social change and Agrarian England 1660–1900.* Cambridge University Press, 1987, p.67–103.
13. King, Peter. 'Legal change, customary rights and social conflict in late eighteenth century England: the origins of the Great Gleaning Case of 1788', *Law and History Review* 10(1), 1992, p.1–31.
14. Eden, F.M. *The state of the poor ...* 1797. Vol.2, p.137.
15. Shave, Samantha A. *Pauper policies: poor law practice in England 1780–1850.* Manchester University Press, 2017, p.34.
16. Oxley, Geoffrey W. *Poor Relief in England and Wales, 1601–1834.* David & Charles, 1974, p.118.

17. Oxley, op cit, p.112–3.
18. Shave, op cit, p.5.
19. These tend to be high-lighted by pauper letters; cf. below, pp.82–3.
20. Shave, op cit, p.127–8.
21. For the rest of his comments, see Snell, *Annals,* op cit, p.7–14.
22. Lees, Lynn Hollen. *The Solidarities of Strangers: The English Poor Laws and the People, 1700–1948.* Cambridge University Press, 1998, p.41 & 113.
23. Freeman, Mark. 'The Agricultural Labourer and the "Hodge" Stereotype, c. 1850–1914', *Agricultural History Review,* 49(2), 2001, p. 172–186.
24. Sharpe, J.A. *Crime in Early Modern England 1550–1750.* 2nd ed. Longman, 1999, p.128.
25. Brundage, Anthony. *The English Poor Laws 1700–1930.* Palgrave, 2002, p.14.
26. Ibid, p.384.
27. Hitchcock, King & Sharpe, op cit, p.12.
28. Cameron, Wendy, Haines, Sheila, & Maude, Mary McDougall, eds. *English immigrant Voices: Labourers' Letters from Upper Canada in the 1830s.* Montreal: McGill-Queen's University Press, 2000, p.195.
29. Slack, op cit, p.6–7.
30. See Pound, John. *Poverty and vagrancy in Tudor England.* Longman, 1971, p.58–68.
31. Pound, op cit, p.107–8, prints the relevant order of the Lord Mayor and Aldermen.
32. Higginbotham, Peter. *The Workhouse encyclopedia.* History Press, 2012, p.92.
33. For this, see Hindle, Steve. *On the parish? The micro-politics of poor relief in rural England c1550–1750.* Clarendon Press, 2004, p.433–45.
34. Alvey, Norman. *From Chantry to Oxfam: a short history of charity and charity legislation.* British Association for Local History, 1995, p.12.
35. King, Steven. *Poverty and Welfare in England 1700–1850: a Regional Perspective.* ManchesterUniversity Press, 2000, p.20–22.
36. This is the argument of King, S., *Poverty and Welfare,* op cit.
37. Hindle, *On the Parish,* op cit, p.216
38. Oxley, op cit, p.102.
39. Hitchcock & Shoemaker, op cit, p.9.
40. Oxley, op cit, p.18.
41. Slack, op cit, p.18.
42. Hindle, *On the Parish,* op cit, p.271.
43. See below, pp.77–9.
44. Tomkins, Alannah. *The Experience of Urban Poverty 1723–82: Parish, Charity and Credit.* Manchester University Press, 2006, p.38–9.
45. Slack, op cit, p.27.
46. Rose, Michael E. 'Settlement, Removal and the New Poor law', in Fraser, Derek, ed. *The New Poor Law in the Nineteenth Century.* Macmillan Press, 1976, p.25.
47. Smith, Adam. *The Wealth of Nations,* ed. Andrew Skinner. Penguin Books, 1970, p.245.
48. Landau, Norma. 'Who was subjected to the Laws of Settlement? Procedure under the Settlement Laws in eighteenth-century England', *Agricultural History Review,* 43(2), 1995, p.139–59.
49. Lees, op cit, p.29.

50. Ashforth, David. 'The Urban Poor law', in Fraser, op cit, p.145.
51. Rose, op cit, p.35.
52. Lees, op cit, p.36.
53. See also below, pp.83–4. For a detailed guide to these sources see Raymond, Stuart A. *Tracing your Ancestors in County Records: a Guide for Family and Local Historians*. Pen & Sword, 2016.
54. Lees, op cit, p.60.
55. Marshall, J.D. *The Old Poor Law, 1795–1834*. 2nd ed. Macmillan, 1968, p.33.
56. Lees, op cit, p.53.
57. Oxley, op cit, p.80.
58. For the Bristol Corporation, see *Butcher, E.E. Bristol Corporation of the Poor, 1696–1898*. Historical Association, Bristol Branch, 1972. See also below, p.87.
59. For a brief account of the Gloucester Corporation of the Poor, see Ripley, Peter. 'Poverty in Gloucester and its alleviation, 1690–1740', *Transactions of the Bristol & Gloucestershire Archaeological Society* 103, 1985, p.185–99.
60. King, S. *Poverty and Welfare*, p.24.
61. Oxley, op cit, p.88–9.
62. Fowler, Simon. *Workhouse: the People, the Places, the Life behind Doors*. National Archives, 2007, p.46. See also Shave, op cit, p.4.
63. Hitchcock, Tim. 'Paupers and preachers: the SPCK and the Parochial Workhouse Movement', in Davison, Lee, et al., eds. *Stilling the Grumbling Hive: the Response to Social and Economic Problems in England 1689–1750*. Alan Sutton, 1992, p.145. For a full listing of pre-1834 workhouses, with maps, see Higginbotham, *Workhouse*, op cit, p.318–27 & 401–7.
64. Crowther, M.A. *The Workhouse System 1834–1929: the history of an English social institution*. Methuen, 1983, p.24.
65. For the implementation of this act, see Shave, op cit, p.56–110.
66. King, op cit, p.28.
67. Brundage, op cit, p.18–19.
68. Fowler, op cit, p.243.
69. Lees, op cit, p.114.
70. Cited by Fowler, op cit, p.245.
71. Fowler, op cit, p.233.
72. Crowther, op cit, p.7.
73. Brundage, op cit, p.105; Lees, op cit, p.233–8.
74. Englander, David. *Poverty and Poor Law Reform in 19th century Britain, 1834–1914*. Longman, 1998, p.27.
75. Hitchcock, King & Sharpe, op cit, p.13.
76. King, *Poverty & Welfare*, op cit, p.229.
77. Fowler, *Workhouses*, op cit, p.51.
78. King, *Poverty & Welfare*, op cit, p.229.
79. Shave, op cit, p.37.
80. Fowler, op cit, p.136. See also **www.workhouses.org.uk/Stratford OnAvon**
81. Fowler, op cit, p.14–15.
82. Englander, op cit, p.25.
83. Lees, op cit, p.278.
84. Flinn, M.W. 'Medical services under the New Poor Law', in Fraser, op cit, p.45–66.

85. Shave, op cit, p.39.
86. For their creation, see Brundage, op cit, p.71–4.
87. Fowler, *Workhouses*, op cit, p.33.
88. Higginbotham, *Workhouse*, op cit, p.60.
89. Lees, op cit, p.196.
90. Englander, op cit, p.34.
91. Fowler, op cit, p.143.
92. Mr Drouet's Establishment for Pauper Children, Tooting **www. workhouses.org.uk/Drouet/**
93. For a brief introduction to education in Workhouses, see Duke, Francis. 'Pauper education', in Fraser, op cit, p.67–86.
94. Lees, op cit, p.276.
95. Higginbotham, Peter. *Children's Homes: a History of Institutional Care for Britain's Young.* Pen & Sword, 2017, p.198.
96. Higginbotham, *Workhouse*, op cit, p.271.
97. Fraser, Derek, ed. *The New Poor Law in the Nineteenth Century.* Macmillan Press, 1976, p.8.
98. Duke, op cit, p.81.
99. Higginbotham, *Workhouse*, op cit, p.43.
100. For a brief discussion of the Act, see Abel-Smith, Brian. *The Hospitals 1800–1948: a Study in Social Administration in England and Wales.* Heinemann, 1964, p.77–82.
101. Ayers, G.M. *England's first state hospitals and the Metropolitan Asylums Board, 1867–1930.* Wellcome Institute of the History of Medicine, 1971.
102. Fowler, op cit, p.175.
103. Higginbotham, *Workhouse*, op cit, p.94.
104. Horn, Pamela. 'The Emigration of Pauper Children to Canada, 1870–1914', *Genealogists' magazine* 25(10), 1997, p.393–9. Horn notes some means of tracing them.
105. Hodgson, Shirley. *Bristol's Pauper Children: Victorian Education and Emigration to Canada.* Bristol Books, 2017, p.11.
106. Digby, Anne. 'The Rural Poor Law', in Fraser, op cit, p.154; Brundage, op cit, p.100.Unfortunately, few records of this scheme survive. Some relevant documents are printed in Hawkings, David T. *Pauper Ancestors: A Guide to the Records Created by the Poor Laws in England and Wales.* History Press, 2011, p.289–95. See also Higginbotham, *Workhouse*, op cit, p.185–7.
107. Crowther, op cit, p.271.
108. Crowther, op cit, p.57–8 & 63.
109. Figures cited by Crowther, op cit, p.167.
110. Fowler, Simon. *Workhouse: the People, the Places, the Life behind Doors.* National Archives, 2007, p.22.
111. Sharpe, J.A. *Crime in Early Modern England 1550–1750.* 2nd ed. Longman, 1999, p.181–2.
112. Hitchcock, Tim, & Shoemaker, Robert. *London Lives: Poverty, Crime and the Making of a Modern City. 1690–1800.* Cambridge University Press, 2015, p.6.
113. Sharpe, op cit, p.223.
114. Briggs, John, et al. *Crime and punishment in England: an introductory history.* UCL Press, 1986, p.188.

115. The changing nature of crime is considered by Emsley, Clive. *Crime and society in England 1750–1900*. Longman, 1996, p.121–50.
116. Sharpe, op cit, p.260.
117. Hawkings, David T. *Criminal Ancestors: a guide to Historical Criminal Records*. Sutton Publishing, 1992, p.19.
118. For a study of the relationship between poor law and charitable provision for the poor in the eighteenth century, see Tomkins, *Experience*, op cit, p.79–111.
119. Fraser, op cit, p.11.
120. Higginbotham, op cit, p.185.
121. Prochaska, Frank. *The Voluntary Impulse: Philanthropy in Modern Britain*. Faber & Faber, 1988, p.43.
122. Prochaska, op cit, p.48.
123. Prochaska, op cit, p.48–9.
124. No records of pensions granted to individuals are known to survive.
125. Brundage, op cit, p.143.
126. Crowther, M.A. *The Workhouse System, 1834–1929: the history of an English social institution*. Methuen, 1983, p.3.
127. Webb, Sidney & Beatrice. *English poor law history, part II: the last hundred years*. English local government v.8. Frank Cass & Co., 1963, v.2, p.434.
128. This database is likely to be subsumed within Discovery **http://discovery.nationalarchives.gov.uk** sometime in 2019.
129. See Raymond, Stuart A. *Parish Registers: a History and Guide*. Family History Partnership, 2009.
130. See Raymond, Stuart A. *The Census 1801–1911: a Guide for the Internet Era*. Family History Partnership, 2009.
131. For a brief discussion of the work of Mayhew and Booth, see Englander, op cit, p.56–79.
132. Eden, op cit, v.3, p.785–93.
133. These are discussed by Lees, op cit, p.281–7.

Chapter 3: Charities

1. For the uses of probate records, see Raymond, Stuart A. *The Wills of our Ancestors: a Guide for Family and Local Historians*. Pen & Sword, 2012.
2. Beier, A.L. *The Problem of Poverty in Tudor and early Stuart England*. Routledge Falmer, 1983, p.3.
3. For the range of charitable concerns in the sixteenth and seventeenth centuries, see Jordan, W.K. *Philanthropy in England, 1480–1660: a Study of the Changing Pattern of English Social Aspirations*. George Allen & Unwin, 1959, p.40–53.
4. Jones, M.G. *The Charity School Movement: a study of eighteenth century Puritanism in action*. Frank Cass & Co., 1964, p.1 & 346.
5. Jones, op cit, passim.
6. Kidd, Alan. *State, Society and the Poor in Nineteenth-Century England*. Macmillan, 1999, p.68.
7. Beaver, Daniel C., ed. *The Account Book of the Giles Geast Charity, Tewkesbury, 1558–1891*. Bristol & Gloucestershire Archaeological Society 31, 2017.
8. For the following examples, see Hitchcock, Tim, & Shoemaker, Robert. *London Lives: Poverty, Crime and the Making of a Modern City 1690–1800*. Cambridge University Press, 2015, p.258–9.

9. Fowler, Simon. *Workhouses. The People, the Places, the Life behind Doors.* National Archives, 2007, p.42.

10. Fowler, Simon. *Poor law records for Family Historians.* Family History Partnership, 2011, p.47. For denominational records, see the present author's works listed below, note 44.

11. But data from the 17th century suggests that poor relief paid by parishes was greater than charitable relief; cf. Goose, Nigel, et al, eds. *The British Almshouse: new perspectives on philanthropy ca 1400–1914.* FACHRS, 2016, p.7–8.

12. McCord, Norman. The Poor Law and Philanthropy', in Fraser, Derek, ed. *The New Poor Law in the Nineteenth Century.* Macmillan Press, 1976, p.97.

13. Fraser, Derek. 'The Poor Law as a Political Institution', in Fraser, op cit, p.123.

14. Tomkins, Alannah. *Experience,* op cit, p.83–4.

15. Kidd, Alan. *State, Society and the Poor in Nineteenth-Century England.* Macmillan, 1999, p.65.

16. Goose, op cit, p.9.

17. Conversely, some specified that funds should be used instead of rates; cf. Hindle, Steve. *On the parish? The micro-politics of poor relief in rural England c1550–1750.* Clarendon Press, 2004, p.125 & 142–5.

18. Cited by Tomkins, *Experience,* op cit, p.105.

19. For its history, see Humphreys, Robert. *Poor Relief and Charity 1869–1945: The London Charity Organization Society.* New York: Palgrave, 2001. See also Lewis, Jane. *The Voluntary Sector: the State and Social Work in Britain: the Charity Organization Society/Family Welfare Association since 1869.* Edward Elgar, 1995.

20. Englander, David. *Poverty and Poor Law Reform in 19th century Britain, 1834–1914.* Longman, 1998, p.29; Brundage, Anthony. *The English Poor Laws 1700–1930.* Palgrave, 2002, p.116.

21. Lees, Lynn Hollen. *The Solidarities of Strangers: The English Poor Laws and the People, 1700–1948.* Cambridge University Press, 1998, p.271 & 281–7. Lees based her information on abstracts of COS judgements made by Charles Booth, now amongst the Booth Papers (see above, p.133).

22. Prochaska, op cit, p.9.

23. Beaver, op cit, passim.

24. Hindle, *On the Parish,* op cit, p.155–64. For apprenticeship indentures, see below, p.74–7. The Sexey's Hospital archives are held by Somerset Archives.

25. Tomkins, *Experience,* op cit, p.100–101. See Oxfordshire History Centre. Oxford City Archives Q.4.9.

26. Clark, Ann, ed. *Sherborne Almshouse Register.* Dorset Record Society, 17. 2013, p.xiii.

27. Goose, Nigel, et al, eds. *The British Almshouse: new perspectives on philanthropy ca 1400–1914.* FACHRS, 2016, p.9 & 12.

28. Clark, *op cit,* p.xix.

29. Nicholls, Angela. *Almshouses in early modern England: charitable housing in the mixed economy of welfare.* Boydell Press, 2017, p.71 & 90; Goose, op cit, p.15.

30. Clark, op cit, p.xxxix-xl.

31. Ibid, p.xxxix.

32. Curthoys, Judith. 'To Perfect the College …: the Christ Church Almsmen 1546–1888', *Oxoniensia* 1995, p.379–95. Patents are in The National Archives HO 118/4 & 7.

33. Clark, *op cit, passim.*

34. Nicholls, op cit, p.201–2.

35. Somerset Heritage Centre DD\SE/46.

36. Henly, H.R., ed. *The apprentice registers of the Wiltshire Society 1817–1922.* Wiltshire Record Society 51. 1997.

37. It ran the Crispin charity, whose indentures are abstracted in Raymond, Stuart A. 'Crispin Apprentices, part 1. Abstracts from the Crispin Charity Indentures of Exeter's Incorporation of Weavers, Fullers and Shearmen, 1694–1780', *Devon & Cornwall Notes & Queries* 42, 2017–18 , p.25–33, 57–64, 89–96, & 117–25.

38. Ripley, Peter. 'Poverty in Gloucester and its alleviation, 1690–1740', *Transactions of the Bristol & Gloucestershire Archaeological Society* 103, 1985, p.193.

39. This may not have been true everywhere; Tomkins, *Experience,* op cit, p.188–9, suggests that the social distance between charity and pauper apprentices in Oxford was not great.

40. McClure, Ruth K. *Coram's Children: the London Foundling Hospital in the Eighteenth Century.* New Haven: Yale University Press, 1981, p.133. Her name, like those of all Foundling Hospital children, had been changed; she was named after the heroine of Samuel Richardson's novel *Clarissa.*

41. Cited by Higginbotham, Peter. *Children's Homes: a history of Institutional Care for Britain's Young.* Pen & Sword, 2017, p.4.

42. Tomkins, *Experience,* op cit, p.184.

43. Ibid, p.175.

44. For these societies, see the present author's *Tracing your Church of England Ancestors.* Pen & Sword, 2017, p.162–5, *Tracing your Nonconformist Ancestors.* Pen & Sword, 2017, p.71; *Tracing your Roman Catholic Ancestors.* Pen & Sword, 2018, p.149–50.

45. Jones, op cit, p.27.

46. Pugh, Gillian. *London's forgotten children: Thomas Coram and the Foundling Hospital.* Tempus, 2007, p.274.

47. For the wide range of institutions holding Catholic archives, see Raymond, Stuart A. *Tracing your Roman Catholic Ancestors.* Pen & Sword, 2018, p.40–61.

48. McClure, Ruth K. *Coram's Children: the London Foundling Hospital in the Eighteenth Century.* New Haven: Yale University Press, 1981, p.8–9.

49. McClure, op cit, p.8–9.

50. Printed in Hawkings, David T. *Pauper Ancestors: A Guide to the Records Created by the Poor Laws in England and Wales.* History Press, 2011, p.319–26.

51. Kidd, op cit, p.92.

52. Kidd, op cit, p.92.

53. Abel-Smith, op cit, p.10–11.

54. For the specialist hospitals, see Abel-Smith, op cit, p.22–31.

55. Fowler, op cit, p.175.

56. This is likely to be subsumed into Discovery **http://discovery. nationalarchives.gov.uk** in 2019.

57. For its origins, see Harrison, Brian. *Drink and the Victorians: the Temperance question in England 1815–1872.* Faber & Faber, 1971, p.181–4.
58. For a similar organization covering London, see the next entry.
59. Prochaska, op cit, p.55.

Chapter 4: Paupers before 1834: Documenting the Old Poor Law
  1. King, Steven. *Poverty and Welfare in England 1700–1850: a Regional Perspective.* Manchester University Press, 2000, p.22.
  2. Hitchcock, Tim, & Shoemaker, Robert. *London Lives: Poverty, Crime and the Making of a Modern City 1690–1800.* Cambridge University Press, 2015, p.287–8.
  3. Lees, Lynn Hollen. *The Solidarities of Strangers: The English Poor Laws and the People, 1700–1948.* Cambridge University Press, 1998, p.49.
  4. For some examples of certificates, see London Lives **www.londonlives.org**
  5. Apprenticed for a shorter period than the usual seven years.
  6. Hembry, Phyllis, ed. *Calendar of Bradford-on Avon settlement examinations and removal orders, 1725–98.* Wiltshire Record Society, 46. 1990, p.37.
  7. Sources for clandestine marriages are discussed by Benton, T. *Irregular marriage in London before 1754.* Society of Genealogists, 1994.
  8. Hitchcock, Tim, & Black, John, eds. *Chelsea Settlement and Bastardy Examinations 1733–1766.* London Record Society 33. 1999, p.83.
  9. Rose, op cit, p.26.
  10. Landau, Norma. 'Who was subjected to the Laws of Settlement? Procedure under the Settlement Laws in eighteenth-century England', *Agricultural History Review,* 43(2), 1995, p.139–59.
  11. London Lives 1690–1800: Settlement **www.londonlives.org/static/Settlement.jsp**
  12. Fowle, J.P.M., ed. *Wiltshire Quarter Sessions and Assizes, 1736.* Wiltshire Archaeological and Natural History Society Records Branch, 11. 1955, p.16–17.
  13. Paley, Ruth. *My Ancestor was a Bastard: a family historian's guide to sources for Illegitimacy in England and Wales.* Rev. ed. Society of Genealogists Enterprises, 2011, p.6.
  14. Wiltshire & Swindon History Centre A1/110/T1684, 128.
  15. Quaife, G.R. *Wanton Wenches and Wayward Wives: peasants and illicit sex in early seventeenth century England.* Croom Helm, 1979, p.203.
  16. For a slightly more sympathetic view of early pauper apprenticeship, see Hindle, *On the parish,* op cit, p.191–223.
  17. Hitchcock & Shoemaker, op cit, p.298 & 383.
  18. Higginbotham, Peter. *The Workhouse Encyclopedia.* History Press, 2012, p.18.
  19. Hitchcock & Shoemaker, op cit, p.396.
  20. Hitchcock & Shoemaker, op cit, p.288.
  21. Devon Archives and Local Studies 3483 A/PO 24
  22. *Poor Law Commissioners' Report of 1834* **www.econlib.org/library/YPDBooks/Reports/rptPLC7.html**, paragraph 1.5.1.
  23. Oxley, G.W. 'Overseers Accounts', in Thompson, K.M. *Short guides to records. Second series guides 25–48.* Historical Association, 1997, p.22. But see below, 'lists of paupers'.

24. London Lives 1690 to 1800: Churchwardens and Overseers of the Poor Account Books (AC) **www.londonlives.org/static/AC.jsp**
25. Wiltshire & Swindon History Centre A1/110/1648, 146.
26. Craven, Alex, ed. *The Churchwardens' Accounts of St Mary's, Devizes, 1633–1689*. Wiltshire Record Society 69. 2016, p.xlvi.
27. Ibid, p.130.
28. Ibid, p.133–4.
29. Ibid, p.134.
30. Mattingly, Joanna, ed.. *Stratton Churchwardens' Accounts, 1512–1578*. Devon & Cornwall Record Society new series 60. 2018, p.174.
31. Ibid, p.187.
32. Ibid, p.187.
33. Price, F.D., ed. *The Wigginton constables' book, 1691–1836*. Banbury Historical Society 11. 1971.
34. For a discussion of a few of these, see Hindle, Steve. *On the parish? The micro-politics of poor relief in rural England c1550–1750*. Clarendon Press, 2004, p.133–4 & (for Layston, Hertfordshire) p.140–42.
35. Oxley, Geoffrey W. *Poor relief in England and Wales 1601–1834*. David & Charles, 1974, p.54–5.
36. Shave, Samantha A. *Pauper policies: poor law practices in England, 1780–1850*. Manchester University Press, 1997, p.131.
37. Hitchcock & Shoemaker, op cit, p.382–3.
38. Hindle, *On the Parish*, op cit, p.281.
39. Taylor, James Stephen. 'Voices in the Crowd: The Kirkby Lonsdale Township Letters, 1809–36', in Hitchcock, Time, King, Peter, & Sharpe, Pamela, eds. *Chronicling Poverty: the Voices and Strategies of the English Poor 1640–1840*. Macmillan Press, 1997, p.122.
40. Hitchcock, Tim, & Shoemaker, Robert. *London Lives: Poverty, Crime and the Making of a Modern City 1690–1800*. Cambridge University Press, 2015, p.139. Abstracts can be viewed at London Lives **www. londonlives.org**
41. For a detailed discussion of their records, together with a listing of published order books and rolls, see Raymond, Stuart A. *Tracing your ancestors in County Records: A Guide for Family & Local Historians*. Pen & Sword, 2016. This volume also discusses the records of Assizes, which occasionally heard poor law cases.
42. Bund, J.W.Willis, ed. *Worcestershire County Records. Division 1. Documents relating to Quarter Sessions. Calendar of the Quarter Sessions papers vol.1. 1591–1643*. Worcestershire Records and Charities Committee, 1900, p.315.
43. Slocombe, Ivor, ed. *Wiltshire Quarter Sessions Order Book 1642–1654*. Wiltshire Record Society, 67. 2014, p.29.
44. Dawes, M.C.B., ed. *Quarter Sessions records of the County of Somerset, vol. IV. Charles II, 1666–1677*. Somerset Record Society, 34. 1919, p.99.
45. Fowle, J.P.M., ed. *Wiltshire Quarter Sessions and Assizes, 1736*. Wiltshire Archaeological and Natural History Society, 11. 1955, p.22.
46. Fowle, op cit, p.51.
47. Crittall, Elizabeth, ed. *The Justicing Notebook of William Hunt, 1744–1749*. Wiltshire Record Society, 37. 1982, p.38.
48. Some of these are outlined by King, Steven. *Poverty and Welfare in England 1700–1850: a Regional Perspective*. Manchester University Press,

2000, p.3–4. King also provides a much fuller bibliography than can be given here.

Chapter 5: Paupers after 1834: Documenting the New Poor Law

1. See, for example, *Chippenham Union Miscellany*. Eureka Partnership, 2016, passim.
2. For coroners' records, see Gibson, Jeremy, & Rogers, Colin. *Coroners' records in England and Wales*. 3rd ed. Family History Partnership, 2009.
3. Hawkings, David T. *Pauper Ancestors: A Guide to the Records Created by the Poor Laws in England and Wales*. History Press, 2011, p.85 & 88.
4. Lees, Lynn Hollen. *The Solidarities of Strangers: The English Poor Laws and the People, 1700–1948*. Cambridge University Press, 1998, p.260.
5. *Chippenham Union Miscellany*. Eureka Partnership, 2016, p.43.
6. Ibid, p.49.
7. These should not be confused with the certified industrial schools, intended for children thought to be in danger of becoming criminals.
8. Lees, op cit, p.333.
9. Quoted by Higginbotham, Peter. *The Workhouse encyclopedia*. History Press, 2012, p.300.
10. *Chippenham Union Miscellany*. Eureka Partnership, 2016.
11. **www.childrenshomes.org.uk/TSExmouth**
12. Higginbotham, *Workhouse*, op cit, p.302.
13. Crowther, op cit, p.75.
14. Hawkings, op cit, p.102.
15. Some local authorities and charities sponsored inoculation at an earlier date. See, for example, South, Mary L., ed. *The Inoculation Book, 1774–1783*. Southampton Records Series 47. 2014. This lists the names of many poor who were inoculated.
16. *Chippenham Union Miscellanea*. Eureka Partnership, 2016, p.52.
17. *Alderbury Union Miscellany*. Eureka Partnership, 2016.
18. Gibson, Jeremy, et al. *Poor Law Union records*. 2nd/3rd eds. 4 vols. Federation of Family History Societies / Family History Partnership, 1997–2014. A listing is included in the introductions to each of the first three volumes.
19. A major project to study pauper letters is currently (2019) in progress at Leicester University; see 'In their Own Write' **www2.le.ac.uk/projects/own-write**
20. Howell, Gary. 'For I was tired of England Sir: English Pauper Emigrant Strategies, 1834–60', *Social History* 23(2), 1998, p.184.
21. Hawkings, op cit, p.163.
22. Hawkings, op cit, p.316.

Chapter 6: Vagrants

1. Eccles, Audrey. 'Vagrancy in later eighteenth-century Westmorland: a social profile', *Cumberland and Westmorland Antiquarian and Archaeological Society transactions* 89, 1989, p.254–5; Eccles, Audrey. *Vagrancy in Law and Practice under the Old Poor Law*. Ashgate, 2012, p.67.
2. Eccles, Audrey. *Vagrancy in law and practice under the Old Poor Law*. Ashgate, 2012, p.133.
3. Hitchcock, Tim, & Shoemaker, Robert. *London Lives: Poverty, Crime and the Making of a Modern City 1690–1800*. Cambridge University Press, 2015, p.309–10.

4. Hindle, On the Parish, op cit, p.306.
5. Sharpe, J.A. *Crime in Early Modern England 1550–1750*. 2nd ed. Longman, 1999, p.142–5.
6. Cited by Beier, A.L. *The Problem of the Poor in Tudor and early Stuart England*. Routledge Falmer, 1983, p.30.
7. Hitchcock, David. *Vagrancy in English Culture and Society, 1650–1750*. Bloomsbury, 2016, p.26.
8. Beier, A.L. *Masterless men*, op cit, p.74.
9. Beier, A.L. *Masterless men*, op cit, p.14.
10. Rose, Lionel. *Rogues and Vagabonds: Vagrant Underworld in Britain 1815–1985*. Routledge, 1988, p.9.
11. Rose, op cit, p.108.
12. Beier, *Masterless men*, p.39.
13. Cited by Beier, *Masterless men*, op cit, p.55.
14. Cited by Beier, *Masterless men*, p.10.
15. Rose, op cit, p.37.
16. Rose, op cit, p.136.
17. Carew, Richard. The Survey of Cornwall, ed. John Cynoweth, Nicholas Orme, & Alexandra Walsham. Devon& Cornwall Record Society new series 47. 2004, p.67.
18. Beier, *Masterless men*, op cit, p.64.
19. Fowler, Simon. 'Vagrancy in mid-Victorian Richmond, Surrey', *Local Historian* 21(2), 1991, p.67.
20. Romani Gypsies in sixteenth-century Britain **www.ourmigrationstory. org.uk/oms/romani-gypsies-in-16th-century-britain**
21. Beier, *Masterless Men*, op cit, p.162–4. See also below, p.XXXXX
22. Eccles, op cit, p.256.
23. Cited by Eccles, *Vagrancy in Law*, op cit, p.164, and by Hitchcock, Tim, & Shoemaker, Robert. *London Lives: Poverty, Crime and the Making of a Modern City. 1690–1800*. Cambridge University Press, 2015, p.240.
24. Hitchcock & Shoemaker, op cit, p.246–7.
25. Hitchcock & Shoemaker, op cit, p.387–8.
26. Hitchcock, *Vagrancy in English Culture*, op cit, p.106 & 111.
27. Eccles, *Vagrancy in Law*, op cit, p.3.
28. Beier, *Masterless men*, op cit, p.32.
29. Cited by Hitchcock, *Vagrancy in English Culture*, p.113.
30. Hitchcock, *Vagrancy in English Culture*, p.137.
31. Eccles, Audrey. 'Vagrancy in later eighteenth-century Westmorland: a social profile', *Cumberland and Westmorland Antiquarian and Archaeological Society transactions* 89, 1989, p.250. For out of place female domestic servants, see Rogers, Nicholas. 'Policing the Poor in Eighteenth-century London: the Vagrancy Laws and their Administration', *Histoire Sociale / Social History*, 24, 1991, p.133–5.
32. Eccles, op cit, p.253.
33. Beier, *Masterless men*, op cit, p.31.
34. Hitchcock, Tim. 'Vagrant lives', in McEwan, Joanne, & Sharpe, Pamela, eds. *Accommodating Poverty: the Housing and Living Arrangements of the English Poor, c.1600–1850*. Palgrave Macmillan, 2011, p.133–5.
35. For an example of a register of badgers' licences and recognizances, see Johnson, H.C., ed. *Wiltshire County Records: Minutes of Proceedings*

in Sessions 1563 and 1574 to 1592. Wiltshire Archaeological & Natural History Society Record Branch 4. 1949, p.1–14.

36. Hitchcock, Tim. 'Vagrant lives', in McEwan, Joanne, & Sharpe, Pamela, eds. *Accommodating Poverty: the Housing and Living Arrangments of the English Poor, c.1600–1850.* Palgrave Macmillan, 2011, p.129.

37. Eccles, Audrey. 'Pretending to be seafaring men: Vagrancy Laws and Forgery with special reference to eighteenth-century Dorset', *Proceedings of the Dorset Natural History and Archaeological Society* 133, 2012, p.1–8.

38. Beier, *Masterless men,* op cit, p.160.

39. Eccles, *Vagrancy in law,* op cit, p.32–3.

40. Price, F.D., ed. *The Wigginton Constables' Book 1691–1836.* Banbury Historical Society 11. 1971, p.83.

41. Hitchcock, *Vagrancy in English Culture,* op cit, p.100.

42. Hitchcock, *Vagrancy in English Culture,* op cit, p.115.

43. Vagrant examinations are analysed in detail by Beier, *Masterless men,* op cit, passim.

44. Ellis, *Vagrancy in law,* op cit, p.141–2.

45. Rose, op cit, p.12 & 14.

46. Slack, Paul A. 'Vagrants and vagrancy in England 1598–1644', *Economic History Review* 27(3), 1974, p.360.

47. Slack, Paul, ed. *Poverty in Early Stuart Salisbury.* Wiltshire Record Society 31. 1975, p.19.

48. Slack, 'Vagrants and vagrancy', op cit, p.361.

49. Eccles, *Vagrancy in Law,* op cit, p.5.

50. Eccles, Audrey. 'The Adams' father and son, vagrant contractors to Middlesex, 1757–94', *London & Middlesex Archaeological Society Transactions* 57, 2007, p.85. These documents are in London Metropolitan Archives.

51. Cited by Crowther, M.A. *The Workhouse System 1834–1929: the history of an English social institution.* Methuen, 1983, p.247.

52. Rose, op cit, p.138 & 145.

53. Legislation touching on this included the Pauper Inmates and Discharge Regulation Act 1871, and the Casual Poor Act 1882.

54. Fowler, op cit, p.67–8.

55. Hunter, Dick. 'Vagrancy in the East and West Ridings of Yorkshire during the late Victorian Period', *Local Historian* 36(3), 2006, p.86.

56. Briggs, John, et al. *Crime and punishment in England: an introductory history.* UCL Press, 1986, p.150.

57. Ibid, p.197.

58. Higginbotham, Peter. *The Workhouse Encyclopedia.* History Press, 2012, p.50.

Chapter 7: Criminals: the Process of Conviction

1. For more information on prosecution, see: London Lives 1690–1800: Prosecutors and Litigants **www.londonlives.org/static/Prosecutors Litigants.jsp**

2. Wiltshire & Swindon History Centre A1/110/T1648, 114.

3. Wiltshire & Swindon History Centre A1/110/T1626.

4. Wiltshire & Swindon History Centre A1/110/T1666.

5. Sharpe, J.A. *Crime in Early Modern England 1550–1750.* 2nd ed. Longman, 1999, p.55–6.

6. Emsley, Clive. *Crime and society in England 1750–1900.* 2nd ed. Longman, 1996, p. 185.
7. Raymond, Stuart A. *Tracing your Ancestors in County Records: a guide for family and local historians.* Pen & Sword, 2016, p.74–8.
8. Wiltshire & Swindon History Centre 383/955.
9. For a fuller listing, see Raymond. *County Records,* op cit, p.49–50.

Chapter 8: Criminals: Sentencing and After

1. Briggs, John, et al. *Crime and punishment in England: an introductory history.* UCL Press, 1986, p.158.
2. Hitchcock & Shoemaker, op cit, p.374.
3. Bates, E.H., ed. *Quarter Sessions records for the County of Somerset, vol.1. James I, 1607–1625.* Somerset Record Society, 23. 1907, p.298.
4. For a more detailed description, see Thomas, Terry. *Criminal Records: a database for the Criminal Justice System and Beyond.* Palgrave Macmillan, 2007, p.11–13.
5. Described by Godfrey, Barry S., Cox, David J., & Farrall, Stephen D. *Serious offenders: a historical study of Habitual Criminals.* Oxford University Press, 2010, p.35–6.
6. Hawkings, David T. *Bound for Australia.* Phillimore, 1987, p.52.
7. For records relating to juvenile delinquents in the National Archives, see Cale, Michelle. *Law and Society: an Introduction to Sources for Criminal and Legal History from 1800.* PRO Publications, 1996, p.111–20.
8. Coldham P.W. *Emigrants in Chains: a social history of forced emigration to the Americas of Felons, destitute children, political and religious non-conformists, vagabonds, beggars and other undesirables 1607–1776.* Alan Sutton, 1992, p.1.
9. Published as Sainty, Malcolm R., & Johnson, Keith A., eds. *Census of New South Wales, November 1828.* Sydney: Library of Australian History, 1980.
10. Hawkings, David T. *Bound for Australia.* Phillimore, 1987, p.74.
11. For a full listing of convict hulk registers, see Hawkings, David T. *Bound for Australia.* Phillimore, 1987, p.230–33.
12. See also HO 7/3.

Chapter 9: Debtors and Bankrupts

1. Innes, Joanna. 'The King's Bench Prison in the later eighteenth century: law, authority and order in a London Debtors' Prison', in Brewer, John, & Styles, John, eds. *An Ungovernable People? The English and their Law in the seventeenth and eighteenth centuries.* Hutchinson, 1980, p.253.
2. Finn, Margot C. *The Character of Credit: Personal Debt in English Culture, 1740–1914.* Cambridge University Press, 2003, p.122 & 124.
3. Finn, *op cit,* p.236.
4. A detailed guide to debtors' prisons throughout the country is included in Neild, James. *An Account of the Rise, Progress and Present State of the Society for the Discharge and Relief of Persons Imprisoned for Small Debts in England and Wales.* Nichols & Son, 1802.
5. Finn, *op cit,* p. 111.
6. Barty-King, Hugh. *The worst poverty: a history of debt and debtors.* Alan Sutton, 1991, p.85–90. Finn, Margot. *The Character of Credit: Personal Debt in English Culture, 1740–1914.* Cambridge University Press, 2003, p.162.

7. Finn, op cit, p.126–7. They are listed in a volume of the Company's signed receipts, 1718–1770. London Metropolitan Archives CLC/L/IB/G/014/MS17009.
8. Finn, op cit, p.163–5.
9. For the 1869 acts, see Finn, op cit, p.186.
10. Finn, op cit, p.187.
11. Bankruptcy and Debtors **www.gloucestershire.gov.uk/media/12220/60-bankruptcy-and-debtors.pdf**
12. Parliamentary Archives HL/PO/JO/10/3/287/7.
13. Finn, *op cit*, p.228.
14. For other records, see Raymond, Stuart A. *Tracing your Ancestors' County Records: a guide for family and local historians*. Pen & Sword, 2016, p.174.
15. Wiltshire & Swindon History Centre A1/120.

Chapter 10: Miscellaneous Sources

1. Wiggins, Ray. *My Ancestor was in the Salvation Army: How can I find out more about them?* 3rd ed. Society of Genealogists Enterprises, 2007, p.41. Some records are held by the Army's International Heritage Centre **www.salvationarmy.org.uk/international-heritage-centre**
2. The most up to date are Raymond, Stuart A. *The Census 1801–1911: a guide for the internet era*. Family History Partnership, 2009; Christian, Peter, & Annal, David. *Census: the family historian's guide*. 2nd ed. National Archives, 2014.
3. These addresses are listed in Higginbotham, Peter. *The Workhouse Encyclopedia*. History Press, 2012, p.328–77. See also **www.workhouses.org.uk/addresses**.
4. Wiltshire & Swindon History Centre, A1/110/ T1662, 151.
5. Devon Heritage Centre 3483 A/PG 1.
6. Wise, Sarah. *Inconvenient People: Lunacy, Liberty, and the Mad-Doctors in Victorian England*. Vintage Books, 2013, p.286.
7. Higginbotham, *Workhouse*, op cit, p.172,
8. *Alderbury Union Miscellany*. Eureka Partnership, 2016, p.17–18.
9. Wiltshire & Swindon History Centre, A1/110/T1648, 165.
10. Ditto, A1/110/T1652, 181.
11. For an introduction, see Raymond, Stuart A. *Parish Registers: a History and Guide*. Family History Partnership, 2009.
12. Tomkins, Alannah. *The Experience of urban poverty, 1723–82: Parish, Charity, and Credit*. Manchester University Press, 2006, p.217.
13. Tebbutt, Melanie. *Making ends meet: pawnbroking and working-class credit*. Methuen, 1984, p.19.
14. Tebbutt, op cit, p.3.
15. Tomkins, op cit, p.210 & 214.
16. This is a revised version of Tomkins, Alannah. 'Pawnbroking and the survival strategies of the urban poor in 1770s York', in King, Stephen, & Tomkins, Alannah. *The Poor in England 1700–1850: an economy of makeshifts*. Manchester University Press, 2003, p.166–98.

INDEX

Personal Name Index

Place Name Index

Subject Index